THE ULTIMATE BOOK OF
CONFIDENCE
TRICKS

THE ULTIMATE BOOK OF
CONFIDENCE

**Boost your
confidence to
an all-time HIGH**

TRICKS

ROS TAYLOR

Vermilion
LONDON

1 3 5 7 9 10 8 6 4 2

First published in the United Kingdom in 2003
by Vermilion, an imprint of Ebury Press
Random House UK Ltd.
Random House
20 Vauxhall Bridge Road
London SW1V 2SA

Random House Australia (Pty) Limited
20 Alfred Street, Milsons Point, Sydney,
New South Wales 2061, Australia

Random House New Zealand Limited
18 Poland Road, Glenfield,
Auckland 10, New Zealand

Random House (Pty) Limited
Endulini, 5A Jubilee Road, Parktown 2193, South Africa

Random House UK Limited Reg. No. 954009
www.randomhouse.co.uk
Papers used by Vermilion are natural, recyclable products
made from wood grown in sustainable forests.

A CIP catalogue record is available for this book from the British Library.

ISBN: 0091884578

Typeset by seagulls

Printed and bound in Great Britain by
Bookmarque Ltd, Croydon, Surrey

CONTENTS

INTRODUCTION
BECOMING VISIBLE

This book will help you become visible, to stand up and be counted, to be noticed for the distinctive contribution you make to life.

Without confidence, you can become like wallpaper – seen but not seen. Lights are hidden under bushels, opportunities ignored, people passed by because they lack the confidence to put themselves forward.

All of us need more confidence. We should all speak up more, complain in a way that brings about results, refuse to be put upon. Every time we are passive to our fate, a little bit of us shrinks and melts away.

Now, please do not believe you have to be instantly bold. If you try that approach, be prepared for setbacks. Teaching someone to change their behaviour suddenly is called 'flooding' by psychologists. This involves, for example, helping a person overcome a fear of spiders by locking them in a room full of spiders. The principle of this is that when anxiety reaches a certain pitch it has to fall, so you become used to the feared object or situation. This is fine when you have a team of people to strap you down. If not, you will probably run for your life and never try again. And who could blame you?

A much better way to go about increasing your confidence is to start small and build. Ko-Ko in *The Mikado* found it difficult to contemplate the beheading of a person, so he resolved to start with the smallest of guinea pigs and work his way up 'the phylogenetic scale'. There is no magic wand for all of this, only a mixture of large and small successes and a gradual build-up of confidence.

Building your confidence has major implications for:

◆ self-esteem, health and wellbeing
◆ close relationships
◆ family
◆ friendships
◆ working life

In his book *Learned Optimism*, Martin Seligman talks of an epidemic of depression. He describes studies in America, but there are similar recent findings in Britain, which show that there has been a tenfold increase in depression during the last century. And over the next decade, suicide will be the major cause of premature death for young men. This is scary stuff.

So what is causing this rise in depression? According to Seligman people have learned to be helpless. They see events in their lives as uncontrollable and this leads to defeat and failure. He talks about an experiment where two groups of rats received electric shocks. The first group could press a bar and the shocks stopped but the second group had no control over the shocks. This group learned to be helpless and gave up even when placed in new situations. They just sat and didn't even try to escape.

So it is with humans. If we learn that our actions make a difference, we are immunised from the effects of depression. The earlier in life this happens the better.

The fantastic news is that confidence reverses fortunes. June Brown from the Institute of Psychiatry carried out some research on the effect of confidence workshops on depressed people. In comparison with a group who received no help, the group who attended the workshops had a significant decrease in anxiety and depression. So this stuff works!

It has taken researchers a long time to convince the medical profession that psychological states can influence physical wellbeing. Years ago at a psychology conference I heard H.J. Eysenck talk about behaviour and health. He claimed to have discovered certain behavioural traits that correlated not only with coronary heart disease but also with cancer. The former was identified with competitiveness and anger; the latter with an inability to express emotion. The most controversial claim was that with a relatively small input from a psychologist – some six group sessions of an hour's duration – people with these traits could be helped to change. What audacity to maintain that you did not require extensive psychotherapy to achieve dramatic successes. Eysenck then went on to suggest that these interventions could add 10 to 15 years to a lifespan. He was pilloried in the medical press, but now some 15 to 20 years later he has been proven correct.

This book will cover all aspects of confidence building,

such as speaking out, influencing your career, challenging your thoughts and emotions as well as becoming active to prevent any chance of depression. And in so doing it could add 10 to 15 years to your life. How exciting! Complete the following quiz to get a flavour of your current confidence levels.

CONFIDENCE QUIZ

1. When confronted with something new like speaking to a 100 people at your local council meeting do you...

a try to avoid such things like the plague?

b say you will think about it to give yourself time to prepare so you don't make a fool of yourself?

c say yes and to hell with the consequences?

2. When thinking about your life – past, present and future – do you believe that...

a excitements are a thing of the past?

b the best is yet to come?

c you would like to do more but can't summon the energy to get up and go?

3. What sort of people do you admire?

a Those who are happy with their lot.

b Those who are constantly striving for something better.

c People who are good looking.

4. Turning up to a party in fancy dress to discover you have misread the invitation and are the only one so attired, would you...

a turn around and go home?

b change in the toilet?

c enjoy being different?

5. When reviewing your friendships over the years, are they...

a ones you have had since schooldays?

b ones you have made relatively recently?

c a mixture of both?

6. If you attended an interview for a promotion and failed, would you...

a just want to die with embarrassment?

b never try that kind of thing again?

c put it down to experience and try again?

7. How do you rate your knowledge and experience?

a You have learned all you need to know to have a good life.

b You would love to do a course but you have always hated anything to do with education.

c You are constantly signing up for courses and travelling to new places.

8. Do you view the future with feelings of...

a excitement?

> **b** dread?
>
> **c** just more of the same?

COMMENTS

1 If you chose (a) and generally tend to avoid challenges then you are choosing to limit yourself. Answers (b) and (c) are equally helpful as your response to the challenge depends on your personality. Taking time to think, plan or acquire new skills is fine but at some point you must 'just do it'.

2 One of the main ingredients for a long active life is mental stimulation. If you feel that excitements are a thing of the past then make a decision to change that right now. And if you feel you lack the energy remember that action precedes change. In other words, you have to start doing things before you feel different.

3 It is worth asking yourself if the people you admire challenge your expectations or make you feel comfortable with your lot. The latter will fail to help you move forward. If they are just beautiful people perhaps you need to learn to look beyond the superficial to the qualities and talents beneath.

4 This situation happened to a client of mine who had been referred to me because she was socially phobic. She went to a Hawaiian party in a bikini and grass skirt to discover that she was the only one. It was her worst nightmare. Initially, she wanted the ground to swallow her up then she thought of going home, but as she stood at the entrance she decided to be bold and laughed and chatted to everyone there. She was such a hit she had six offers of dates. **Bold works.**

5 If you chose to answer (a) then it is more power to you that you have maintained these friendships over the years and if (b) then perhaps you have a great capacity for making friends wherever you are. The combination of old and new reveals a commitment to the past but also a desire to meet the new.

6 Failure is always discomfiting but from it you learn. If you feel such embarrassment that you cease taking risks then you stop moving forward. Feel foolish if you have to then pick yourself up and try again.

7 Comfort and security are great, but learning at any age will help you know you are alive. Having goals to learn a new language, meet new people or travel to distant places lifts the spirits and helps life to stay exciting.

8 If you face the future with dread (b) or if you feel it will be humdrum (c) then now is the time to surprise yourself with a new skill, a new job or some expansion of your horizons. Confidence tricks will help.

IT'S EASIER THAN YOU THINK

I am not suggesting you become something you are not. As you progress through this book you will discover **reality checks** where you are invited to become aware of any issues of confidence. The positive-thinking lobby has created a lot of dissatisfaction as people of negligible talent pursue their fragment of fame almost as a human right. They then become profoundly dissatisfied as they reach for quite unattainable goals. The secret is knowing yourself and your positive attributes, and playing to these strengths. Weaknesses can then be worked upon or dismissed.

Psychological research reveals that lack of confidence is a habit, like biting your nails or eating too much. So the method for overcoming this habit will be similar to any other.

First you must change your **thinking** about your lack of confidence, whatever that might be, then tackle any negative **feelings** to turn them into powerful, progressive ones and finally take **action** to behave differently. Each chapter will deal with these three aspects so you can become an expert in your issues and your life.

There is a questionnaire for you to answer at the beginning of every chapter to prompt you into reviewing that particular part of your life and provide you with a reality check about what you need to do to gain more confidence. It also allows you to see at a glance the particular areas of confidence you need to work on so that you can create your own **confidence boosting activity plan**.

Chapter one tackles confidence on the inside. It focuses on the intangible quality of confidence – inner confidence or self-esteem. Looking the part is also important and tricks of the body language trade will be shared so that, when all else fails, you can bluff your way to confidence. Nothing wrong with that! The successful do it all the time.

Chapter two is about confidence with lovers and partners and will also deal with the 'F' word – feelings. For many people it is anathema to talk about their feelings, but confidence levels are entirely entwined with emotional expression. How can anyone possibly ignore them? People do, of course, but I will show you ways in which you can 'learn the language' of emotions. Talking freely about emotions takes confidence and this chapter provides the tools. Meeting, mating, marriage, making up and breaking up will all be covered.

Chapter three addresses confidence with your family. We often fight against 'turning out like our parents', only to end up catching ourselves saying and doing the same things. This chapter offers specific suggestions as to how you can be different, confounding your genetic inheritance. Part of this chapter will deal with adults grappling with confidence issues in the face of their own backgrounds but will also deal with parental issues – the reader as parent.

Chapter four deals with confidence and friendship. Petty jealousies can undermine confidence and eventually undermine friendships. In this chapter I will provide confidence techniques to help you make friends, keep friends and be assertive in difficult situations.

The last chapter, Chapter five, looks at confidence in the workplace. It covers all the issues that will help you to become more successful at work, starting with assessing your strengths and facing your weaknesses. Volunteering for projects, speaking up at meetings, presenting your ideas and feeling comfortable at interviews all increase your confidence.

The best way to approach this book is to view yourself as an experiment. Experimentation is the rational process of establishing what does and doesn't work, with no emotion involved. As you begin to see yourself as a project, you can distance yourself from your past and any old ways of doing things.

I gave a card to a friend recently which said 'Freedom lies in being bold'. Now is your time to be bold.

1

CONFIDENCE ON THE INSIDE

What is confidence on the inside? And how will you know it when you get it?

People often ask me for my definition of self-confidence when I speak at conferences or chat at book signings. My definition includes the ability to be yourself and to go anywhere and try anything in a positive fashion without fear or embarrassment. It is also the pursuit of your dreams, the growth of your talents and the self-esteem to believe that you deserve success.

Nelson Mandela quoted Marianne Williamson in his inaugural speech in 1994. She says *'our greatest fear is not that we are inadequate but that we are powerful beyond measure...Your playing small does not serve the world. There is nothing enlightened about shrinking so that other people won't feel insecure around you.'*

So holding back on what you can offer the world, hiding your light under a bushel, is the opposite of confidence. You know you are confident when you volunteer for a challenge and do not even entertain the possibility of failing.

Before you can start to increase your confidence, however, you must get to know yourself and some of those unhelpful habits you have acquired. Answer the questions below as honestly as possible. This assessment has no right or wrong answers and no perfect score.

REALITY-CHECK YOURSELF

1. Do you think positively about yourself and others? ....
If not, why not?..

2. Are you a worrier? ....
If yes, what do you worry about?...............................

3. Would you consider yourself to be lucky? ....

4. If you are upset or angry can you deal with these emotions by speaking directly to the people involved? ....

5. Can you be assertive in most situations? ....

6. Can you simply relax and do nothing without feeling guilty? ....
If not, why not?...

7. Do you get enough sleep? ....

8. Do you take enough holidays? ....
If not, why not?...

9. Do you watch too much TV – more than two
hours a night?...

10. Do you allow time for yourself?
If not, why not?...

11. Are the activities you take part in chosen by you
or by others? ....
If the latter, why?...

12. Can you go out by yourself to a restaurant or
a cinema?..
If not, why not?...

13. Can you enter a room full of strangers without
feeling uncomfortable?...

RATING YOUR ANSWERS
Questions 1 to 3: Your Thinking Style

Your thinking style is the very bedrock of confidence. If you are
a negative thinker, you will tend to have low self-esteem,
which in turn will affect your levels of confidence. We will be
looking at thinking at length in this chapter.

Worrying is a form of negative thinking and is singularly unsuccessful at helping you achieve what you desire. If you answered yes to question 2 then you need to make that a goal for change.

Research by psychologists like Martin Seligman reveals that you make your own luck. The more persistent you are, the luckier you get.

Questions 4 to 8: Emotions and Energy

An ingredient of confidence is the ability to handle strong feelings in a purposeful way so that you can solve issues speedily. Standing up for what you believe in in a way that is not offputting to others is very much a confidence skill.

Question 5 is crucial to confidence. If you can assert yourself in as pleasant a way as possible in most situations, you can progress through life boldly.

Some people just have to be on the go all the time, spending every second engaged in purposeful activity. Sitting and doing nothing for short periods helps you to wind down. If you are relaxed you are more in control and likely to feel confident.

There are times when lack of sleep is unavoidable. For example, if you have a young baby, are studying for exams or trying to meet a deadline. However, getting a good night's sleep is important for wellbeing and confidence.

Holidays need not be expensive trips abroad but they do have to be different from everyday routine. This break relaxes you and restores energy. Life without a break becomes a drudge.

So if you have answered no to questions 4 to 8, add these to your goal list.

Questions 9 to 13: Actions and Behaviour

If you answered yes to question 9 then you are watching too much television and need a variety of more stimulating activities.

Question 10 identifies that making time for yourself creates a feeling of self-worth, which is so important for confidence. Question 11 deals with pursuing your own interests as well as accommodating those around you. This is also part of forming your own identity and building confidence. Going out on your own, without the comfort of friends and family, can be a challenge, but your confidence increases exponentially if you can achieve that independence. Walking through that door into a room full of strangers can be a trial for even the most confident of us. If you can conquer that fear, however, you are well on the way to becoming confident.

So if you have answered no to any of the questions between 9 and 13, add them to your goals for change.

Use this chapter like a recipe book. Dip into the tricks that will work for you. It is organised around thinking, feeling and doing because that is the psychological process to achieving personal change.

CONFIDENCE SAPPERS

Let us first explore the reasons why you might lack confidence. Areas that immediately come to mind as potential confidence sappers are:

◆ close relationships
◆ family
◆ school and peer groups
◆ work

RELATIONSHIPS

Any relationship in which you feel stuck or helpless will undermine confidence. A pilot attended my clinic for psychological help as he feared he was going to fail his exams for the 757. Flight training is very specific to aircraft type and he would not be able to fly 757s, which are used on domestic routes, until he passed. The problem was that this previously confident man was panicking about these exams. Subsequent sessions revealed that he was having arguments with his wife, who hated his life as a pilot. He looked cowed and battered and was sleeping badly. Discussions centred around finding an amicable way of living with his wife or separating from her. At a final session he seemed less anxious and flight training was progressing.

Imagine my surprise when I was flying to Scotland some time later to hear a familiar voice saying 'This is your Captain, John Smith, welcoming you on this 757 flight to Edinburgh.' Normally a very relaxed flier, I felt I had to check out the flight deck on this one. But what a different man greeted me. Relaxed, confident, exams passed (checked that one) and, since his divorce, a new girlfriend to meet him at the airport.

Bad relationships can severely sap your confidence.

FAMILY

There is no doubt that the family you are born into does make a difference. Professor Gordon Claridge conducted a number of twin studies over a long period to determine the influence of upbringing versus genetics. Studying identical twins brought up separately allows psychologists to explore how much behaviour is learned and what is intrinsic. These studies revealed that if one or both of your genetic parents lacked confidence then you have a 60 to 80 per cent chance of being the same. But although genetics have a profound influence, and it is better in terms of outcome to instil confidence at an early age, there is still a 20 to 40 per cent leeway for change.

Literature is teeming with stories of late developers. Look at Mary Wesley, who became an author when she was 70. It is so important to realise that you can change if you have the desire and the knowledge of how to go about it.

Many of the people I coach have the false notion that you pop out of the womb perfectly formed, and they will utter the phrase 'well you can't change the way you basically are'.

Well, yes you can! Of course there are bits of you that are immutable, like whether you are introverted or extroverted, but much of the rest is up for grabs. All human beings are capable of so much more than they think.

SCHOOL AND PEER GROUPS

If school and peer groups make children feel defeated and failures, the effects of this can last a lifetime. Nigel in the programme 'Confidence Lab', a BBC2 series I was involved in, was profoundly affected by a teacher telling him that he was useless at writing. It had held him back in his career because managers were required to write reports and he feared that if he were promoted to manager, it would be discovered that he could not write. After he went for help with his writing skills, word spread about his new-found confidence to the extent that he was headhunted no less than three times for managerial posts. He didn't even have to apply!

WORK

The BBC carried out a work survey prior to the launch of their Get Confident website in March 2001 and discovered that 81 per cent of people who responded had never asked for promotion and 51 per cent had never asked their boss for a pay rise. This reluctance was misplaced, as over three-quarters of those who did speak up received more money or that sought-after promotion.

The press release was entitled 'Quiet Britons miss out on promotion'. You can just imagine a country seething with unfulfilled ambition because the majority lack the confidence to ask for what they want.

The other piece of the work puzzle is that managers do not always encourage freedom of thought and speech at work. In their book *Unshrink*, Max McKeown and Philip Whiteley discuss this desire for conformity from those at the head of large organisations and the effect this has on employees.

Their thesis is that work, rather than stretching and enhancing us, often has quite the opposite effect. Managers expect us to obey orders mindlessly and serve the god of money at all costs, which in turn shrinks us as individuals. That may sound a little overstated but the increase in stress-related absence and litigation over the last two or three years bears significant testimony to overly long hours worked and the advent of a bullying managerial style in the workplace.

We will talk more about how to avoid these kinds of companies in Chapter 5. But speaking up about what you believe in and what you want is as essential as breathing. And although a job is important, your sanity is more so.

CONFIDENCE SAPPERS ZAPPERS

Follow the three steps below and notice the difference in your life.

STEP 1: IDENTIFY THAT SAPPED FEELING

If you have experienced the following feelings, you have been sapped:

◆ You felt good about yourself till you met this person. Then you felt unaccountably depressed.

◆ Anything you can do they can do better till you just want to scream.

◆ You feel criticised, directly or indirectly, by most of their comments.

◆ You spend too much time talking to others about this confidence-sapping relationship.

◆ You feel supported by them only when you are upset or needy so they can feel in charge.

STEP 2: IDENTIFY THE SAPPER

You must identify the person or people who steal your energy. Check the list below to prompt your thinking.

Spouse or partner	Grandparents
Male friend	Mother
Female friend	Father
Teacher/lecturer	Brother
Boss	Sister
Colleagues	Boyfriend
Neighbours	Girlfriend
Other relatives	

STEP 3: ZAP THE SAPPER

Choose to take action in at least one of the following ways:

◆ Limit contact so that you spend less time in their company. This could be difficult if you are married to them.

◆ Spend more time with people who make you feel good about yourself.

◆ Ask the sapper to be more positive and/or supportive.

◆ As soon as you feel sapped, become really positive and energetic. Sappers hate that.

◆ Refute any criticism openly.

◆ Ask the sapper if they are OK because you detect that they might be more negative than usual.

◆ Just refuse to let them get to you even in your quieter moments.

CONFIDENT THINKING

Confidence on the inside is so much about how you think. There are many ways of thinking that can help propel you towards a more confident future or the pitfalls of pessimism.

Confident people think of themselves as winners and as lucky people. When I interviewed 80 chief executives for my last book *Fast Track to the Top*, my final question was 'to what do you attribute your success?' After talking extensively about the skills that rocketed them to success, the majority then answered that it had all been due to luck. I remember feeling slightly irritated by this response, as surely these business leaders realised that their own endeavours had promoted their rise to the top. Surely they could not believe it was all due to serendipity. On reflection, however, it occurred to me that they simply saw themselves as lucky winners.

Over many years working as a psychologist, I have discovered that there are certain thinking styles associated with pessimism and feelings of failure and others with confidence and success. I have outlined some **pessimist pitfalls** next so that you can identify which thinking style might be yours. There is an **antidote** for each to offer you the option of **optimism**.

PESSIMIST PITFALL: 1
'Bad things always happen to me'

If you believe that life will deliver blows no matter what you do, you are more likely to give up easily and feel helpless in the face of a crisis. I call it **always bad thinking**.

I was speaking recently to a volunteer in a hostel for the homeless. She told me that when she met the young people prior to entering the hostel, they were full of hope and expectations for the future but by the time they had been in the hostel for two weeks and met the other long term inmates, they started talking about feeling stuck and never getting a chance to get out of the rut. They had become permanent pessimistic thinkers, just like the rest. She described them as lethargic and hopeless. They had acquired 'always bad thinking.'

A quick check to see if you indulge in 'always bad thinking' is becoming aware of using words like 'always' and 'never'. Other examples are:

◆ 'You never want to do what I want.'
◆ 'Diets never work.'
◆ 'I am always in such a mess.'

The Antidote

Now, on the other hand, if you believe that a bad event is just a temporary setback then you will bounce back and regain your optimism. This is **sometimes bad thinking**. Examples are:

◆ 'I know you like to do your own thing but it would be great if you could do what I want sometimes.'

◆ 'Diets don't work for me when I am tired. When I relax, it will be effective.'

◆ 'I am in a mess just now but I will get sorted out soon.'

PESSIMISTIC PITFALL: 2
'What I did worked today but with my luck I bet it won't work tomorrow'

Attributing good events to temporary luck is a sign of super-stitious thinking. We have all heard people say when we compliment them on a success, 'Thanks, but I know it won't last.' This occurs when you are afraid to say that things are going well in case it all falls apart. You may even believe that as soon as you are successful, fate will intervene to keep you humble. Favourite words and phrases are 'with my luck', and qualifiers like 'only' and 'just'.

Superstitious thinking sounds like this:

◆ 'I am only as good as my last success. It may all disap-pear in an instant.'

◆ 'I won just because everyone else dropped out. If I had to do it again, I don't think I could.'

◆ 'I am successful, but only when other people help me out.'

The Antidote

If you believe that you can build on success and that there is no reason why that success should not continue, then you will overcome superstitious thinking. This **winning thinking** is at the heart of optimism and helps people to be in charge of their own fate. It has nothing to do with chance but a lot to do with thinking that you are a winner.

For example, when I left my company to set up entirely on my own, which was more than a little terrifying, my mother said to me, 'Don't worry, something will turn up. It always does.' This was a wonderful example of **winning thinking** which helped me enormously when cash flow was more of a trickle. Some more examples of lucky thinking are:

◆ 'There is no reason why I can't go on to bigger and better things.'

◆ 'I won because of my staying power.'

◆ 'I am really good at motivating others to help create a winning team. Perhaps I can do this for the entire company.'

PESSIMISTIC PITFALL: 3
'I didn't even get that job. I am becoming completely unemployable'

Everywhere thinking involves believing that when one thing happens it affects all areas of your life. In other words if you cut off your head, 'failure' or 'success' would be written right through the centre of your body, like Blackpool rock. You may catastrophise about your future and see your life as being completely ruined. As a result you are more likely to succumb to depression.

Examples of 'everywhere thinking' for bad things happening to you are:

◆ 'I've lost my job. I am a complete failure.'
◆ 'I am utterly unattractive to the opposite sex.'
◆ 'The Government is a total waste of time.'

The Antidote

It is much better to be aware that you have been less than successful in only a specific area than believing you are a total failure. Keeping to specifics means that you can solve problems. As soon as you generalise you get stuck thinking that you can't change and that life is hopeless.

Optimistic Options

◆ Let the good things that happen give the whole of your life an optimistic glow. I remember speaking to the head of competitions at *Reader's Digest*. He said that winning even small amounts of money can change people profoundly as suddenly they see themselves as winners, not just of *Reader's Digest* competitions but in general terms.

◆ See yourself as a winner even in adversity. I am currently working with homeless people. One young homeless man told me his story of being caught apparently breaking and entering a basement apartment. The owner of the house had been woken by a noise. He opened his curtains in the middle of the night to be confronted by this young man standing outside his window. He understandably thought that he was up to no good and called the police. Despite finding no evidence – jemmy, booty or fingerprints – the police arrested him and he was brought to trial. He told me that when asked by the prosecution what he was doing standing outside the window, he replied that he had been sleeping below some steps and stood up to stretch. He went on, he said, to ask whether the barrister, a very plump man who clearly enjoyed the good things in life, had ever slept on the ground, because when you were thin you bruised easily and had to move regularly. Apparently there was an embarrassed silence till the barrister sat down, his cross-examination terminated somewhat prematurely.

The young man told me it took the jury two minutes to dismiss his case. The point of this story is that he looked as if he had won the lottery. He had been on remand for weeks, if not months, and yet that day he was a winner. Some people had believed in him. I was left thinking that the cost of the trial with barristers, a judge and jury would have paid for his university education. Goodness knows what failures were in his background but all changed for him that day.

So a summary would be:

FOR BAD EVENTS

The pessimist thinks they	The optimist thinks they
always	**sometimes**
in every part of their life	**in some circumstances**
will fail in some way	might fare less well

FOR GOOD EVENTS

The pessimist thinks they
sometimes
in specific circumstances
might succeed

The optimist thinks they
always
in every part of their life
will succeed

PESSIMISTIC PITFALL: 4
'It's all my fault'

Personalisation or **me thinking** means that we blame ourselves when bad things happen. You may internalise all that goes wrong when realistically this blame could be directed elsewhere. Low self-esteem follows swiftly.

When you look at the opposite, or **not me thinking**, it may appear positive and optimistic, but is it really? Someone who goes around blaming everyone else for their failures may bolster their ego in the short term. Ultimately, however, this merely stops them looking at themselves truthfully. For me, both of these are unhelpful thinking styles in different ways.

Some examples of 'me thinking' are:

◆ 'It's all my fault.'

◆ 'I have let the team down.'

◆ 'I'm to blame for the failure of my marriage. I just wasn't interesting enough.'

Examples of 'not me thinking' are:

◆ 'It's all their fault.'

◆ 'The team should have covered for me.'
◆ 'My partner was poor marriage material.'

We have all come into contact with people who will blame everyone but themselves. We call them 'slopey shouldered', as they take no responsibility for anything going wrong but are suddenly around when there are accolades. This 'not me thinking' is the stuff of arrogance, the birth of the strut.

For good events, this thinking is reversed. The 'me thinker' is willing to admit that they were successful and it was all down to their efforts. The 'not me thinker', just like at Oscar ceremonies, will always find other people, including the cat, to share the limelight. They are deeply embarrassed when you try to give them a compliment, as their view of themselves does not match your positive statement and they reject it. The 'me thinker', for good events, believes that they deserve to win.

Martin Seligman, the research psychologist, dismisses 'me thinking' as less important than the other two – 'always' and 'everywhere'. He believes the latter determine our actions whereas the former just gives rise to emotion. He says 'it controls only how you feel about yourself'. From my point of view, how you think and then feel about yourself strikes at the very heart of confidence. If we blame ourselves for everything bad that happens to us then we will have such low self-esteem that life becomes an increasingly depressing place. On the other hand, if we blame others all the time, we will have developed little insight, and have a precarious sense of our own self-worth and few strategies in place for the day some-one or some group confronts us.

BALANCED THINKING

So when bad events, situations or relationships happen in our lives, how should we think about them? Taking them personally, believing them to be entirely our fault, is not helpful but neither is blaming everyone else.

Balanced thinking is a cool, rational appraisal of what is going on. When something disastrous happens we naturally become depressed and upset, but the sooner we can come to a realisation about who or what caused the event, what we can do to limit the damage, what the next step is and what we can learn from the whole experience, the quicker we can move forward.

So we are not talking about putting a sticking plaster over the hurt and pretending to be positive. That might pass for help in other books but not this one.

BALANCED THINKING FOR CONFIDENCE IN A CRISIS

1. Evidence

◆ What evidence is there to support your belief that you are to blame?

◆ What evidence is there to support your belief that others are to blame?

◆ Could it be a combination of circumstances? If so, which ones?

2. Alternatives

◆ What friends could you ask to support or refute your analysis? Do you trust them to be unbiased?

◆ What are their views and how do they differ from yours?

◆ What experts do you know in this area who could help you? What could you ask them?

3. Learning

◆ What would you do differently next time?

◆ What have you learnt from the experience?

◆ How do you feel having gone through this process?

4. Action

◆ Who do you have to deal with now to make the situation better?

◆ What must you do to ensure it does not happen again?

◆ How do you rate your confidence now?

The analysis that leads to balanced thinking need not be prolonged. It could be a couple of phone calls and some thinking time. Initially, I would propose that you write down the results. There is something satisfyingly constructive about seeing the contents of your mind in print. It minimises the event and maximises your control.

I used the technique myself recently. I had to decide whether to leave a company I had set up and hand the reins over to others or to stay but feel that it was increasingly not reflecting my values. Were they right and was I wrong or vice versa? Could I survive starting my own business all over again? Could I extricate myself and still keep close relationships with colleagues that I held dear?

I used the analysis above and was amazed to discover that friends, colleagues and experts rated my ability to go it alone greater than I did myself. I realised that much of the current situation was down to me but much could also be attributed to others, so I was not entirely to blame. This helped me to negotiate my departure in a blame-free, amicable way, set up Ros Taylor Ltd and take time to write this book.

BALANCED THINKING AND GENDER DIFFERENCES

It is sad, or perhaps just an interesting fact of life, that women will sometimes be stuck forever at the rumination phase of Balanced Thinking, blaming themselves eternally and never moving on. Men, on the other hand, skip the first three processes and move straight to action. It certainly makes life simple. Lose a pert blonde wife – get another the same as soon as possible so that the first wife will never see any hurt or loss. No self-awareness is developed, nothing is learnt, so mistakes are repeated. Women always believe they can change their man – another sex difference, so there are always other pert blondes waiting round the corner.

There are no rights or wrongs in these differences but they help us to understand what we need to work on. Women need to move on from blame to action. Men need to concentrate on the in-between parts; what blame to accept and what has been learnt.

Why are men and women different? Apart from the obvious reason that it would be a boring life if we were all the same, it seems to be a mixture of nature and nurture. There is no doubt that, neurologically, we are wired differently. Add in the learned behaviour of man as action man and woman as caring and nurturing and 'vive la différence'.

CONCLUSION

To conclude this section, you are more likely to be optimistic if you believe that good things are always happening to you in all parts of your life and you have caused them than if you believe that good things happen only sometimes in a few selected areas of your life and they are generally due to others' interventions.

You are more likely to be pessimistic if you believe bad events always happen to you in every part of your life and you are to blame for everything or you consistently blame others for your mistakes. On the other hand, if you think that bad things occasionally happen only in some parts of your life and these are due to a mixture of circumstances, some caused by you, some not, then you will definitely have the tendency to be optimistic.

Balanced thinking helps you to get a grip on reality and to create your own luck!

WORRY, WORRY, WORRY

Are you the type of person who is always worried about making a social gaffe, saying the wrong thing to their boss, using the wrong knife and fork when eating out? Do you worry more nebulously about what the future will bring? Do you even worry about being or not being worried? If so, you are using what I would call **what if thinking**. You tend to fear the worst, envisaging some calamitous result if you make a social gaffe, sometimes with all the attendant shame that can bring – pink pulsating face, fearing every eye upon you.

There are a couple of mind games to avoid all this and help you become bold and more confident in all areas of your life.

GAME OF CONSEQUENCES

Think of your worst fear or embarrassment. Then, say it came to pass, what would the consequences be? If that happened then what would that lead to? If that came to pass, then what? Indulge your 'what if thinking' to its ultimate goal. Face it and see if it is as bad as you had imagined.

Let me give you an example. I used to sing in opera and always feared forgetting my words. I would have nightmares about it, waking up in a cold sweat. My consequences would go like this:

MY CONSEQUENCES

What if I forget my words?
Then the consequence will be that…
I will freeze to the spot
Then the consequence will be…
The audience will think I am a fool
The consequence of that will be…
I will never be asked to sing again
The consequence of that will be…
I cannot have a career in singing
The consequence will be…
I would have to find something else to do
The consequence of that will be…
OK really – I would always think of something to do.

We rarely face the ultimate outcomes of our fears. If we do confront them we are left saying 'so what?' As soon as I indulged in this mind game I realised that I could make the words up when I sang as the audience rarely had a clue exactly what the words were at the best of times. Because I felt more relaxed I started to enjoy singing much more. The pressure not to make mistakes and to be perfect had disappeared as I realised that I could cope with any adversity. Try your own Consequences below.

Consequences Mind Game

Choose your worst fear or embarrassment to fill in the space.

What if..happened?

Then what would be the consequence ....
....

Then if that happened what would be the consequence.........
....

Then what would be the consequence ....
....

The consequence of that would be ....
....

And the consequence of that would be ....
....

The final consequence of that would be ....
....

So what?

When you have practised this with a number of different scenarios, you can jump the in-between stages and head straight for the 'so what?' That is a sign of confidence, so make it your goal.

WINNING VISUALISATIONS

These are perhaps more a series of games or tricks than a single mind game.

First Winning Visualisation

When I am faced with something to worry about, such as a big presentation to 2,000 people, I will put it out of my mind with a particular image. The one I find helpful is a large brush, the sort you see janitors using, sweeping aside the fluttering leaves of my anxiety. And I say to myself, 'I will worry about that the day before.' When that day comes I sweep aside the leaves and say I will worry about that the hour before and when that arrives I sweep and tell myself to worry about it afterwards – and by then it is too late.

It is strange that I use a domestic analogy to allay my anxiety as I am the least domesticated person you are ever likely to meet and have never been known willingly to handle a brush. But there it is and it works for me. I just know that worry disrupts anything I do and undermines my success. You must choose the image that works for you. It can be any implement that moves or dislodges your worry. It is important that the movement is calm and soothing.

Second Winning Visualisation

I used the second game to great effect at a time when almost everything I did was new, challenging and frightening. I would start the day sitting on the edge of my bed, imagining success at every point. This is what I would say to myself: first meeting going well and they want to listen to me, coffee time and the morning has been a success, next meeting, no problems – they like what I am telling them and now it is lunch so half the day is gone and I am relaxed.

You get the idea. The feelings of dread I would get just disappeared as I began to see myself as more successful.

This is based entirely on the fact that what we dread in our minds rarely comes to pass. These wild imaginings simply stir our anxieties and then we lack the confidence to go boldly through our life.

Third Winning Visualisation

When you are really up against it your anxieties can penetrate your dreams, giving them the quality of nightmares.

I know of friends who have terrifying nightmares of falling off cliffs, or being trapped in burning buildings or crashing cars, all before exams.

For me my terror, as I have mentioned before, was standing on stage, forgetting not only my words but the name of the show or opera as well. I would wake bathed in sweat with the conviction that this was going to be reality.

The way to change all this is to change your dream. Friends have told me that they have sprouted wings and flown across cliffs, parachuted out of burning buildings and accelerated faster than the speed of light from car crashes. All you need to do is program yourself with the additional piece of your dream before you fall asleep.

In my dreams when I was stuck for words or unsure what I was singing, I simply asked the audience. Your solution does not have to be rational. It just gets you out of the situation

So, to recap, indulge in mind games to change wild imaginings to winning visualisations:

◆ Sweep away the leaves of your anxiety (or your own vision).

◆ Imagine every part of the day in advance and see yourself as mastering each step.

◆ Change your dreams/nightmares so that you are in charge. Do this before you fall asleep.

All of these techniques put you in charge of your thoughts.

CIRCULAR THINKING

Another unhelpful thinking habit which dogged me was something I call circular thinking. This used to happen in the middle of the night when I woke up or could not fall asleep. I would worry about something that had happened that day and I would look at it from all angles. This thinking would go round in circles and keep me awake for hours.

I realised that I never resolved anything with this nocturnal thinking but simply made myself more upset, so I invented some rules.

RULES TO STRAIGHTEN OUT THAT CIRCULAR THINKING

◆ Keep a pen and paper beside the bed for this exercise.

◆ If you are awake worrying about issues of the day for more than 20 minutes, get up and write them down in a list.

◆ When you have completed your list, identify the problems you can resolve. Write down the names of people you will need to contact.

◆ If there is nothing you can do, erase that item.

◆ Tell yourself that it will all seem less upsetting in the morning.

◆ Then go to sleep.

I have discovered that writing worries down is therapeutic, as the process extracts the issues and pins them to paper, instantly making them appear more manageable.

If you are in the middle of a crisis and any advice about thinking styles will not come to mind, remember **when all else fails...**

There is a great story about Jesse Jackson, who was trying to help black people in America gain a sense of their own worth. He had them chant at his gatherings, 'I am somebody.'

So if you ever feel like a squashed currant on the floor of life say, 'I am somebody'. You can add 'somebody worthy of respect' or 'somebody who is a winner' or 'somebody who is worth knowing'. Chant it at least three times like a mantra each morning till you believe it.

EMOTIONS

Daniel Goleman, of *Emotional Intelligence* fame, has got us used to the idea that without emotion we are automatons. However, tell that to someone who has just burst into tears during an important meeting. We would all much rather be 'cool' at moments like that, so we must express our emotions appropriately for the situation. For that you need to control and direct your feelings.

We all have different approaches to emotions. I have listed below a number of examples, so work out which way is closest to yours.

1 **You avoid powerful emotions as much as possible. You feel foolish and out of control so you say nothing, hiding behind politeness in the hope that these disruptive feelings will go away. But you do experience strong feelings.**

Many people, especially British people, would do almost anything rather than experience an uncomfortable emotion. And by the same token, they hate any unbridled feeling directed at them; their only response is to placate at any cost. So they miss out on life's glories.

Ron had a very unhappy marriage – he realised he had made a mistake on his wedding night. He did not love his wife and should never have married her. He had a series of affairs, nothing disruptive, nothing that would destroy this shell of a marriage, till he met the woman he really loved. But Ron found this love thing too disruptive too damaging to his view of himself as a pillar of the community. He also feared opprobrium and emotion from his wife, who would be justifiably upset and furious. So it was easier to turn his back on love and regain 'a proper composure'.

2 You deny experiencing any emotion whatsoever. That way you can keep your cool through good times and bad.

Sometimes it is easier to pretend that you don't actually feel anything. You kind of dissociate yourself from the feeling because to face it would mean making profound changes.

Chris was constantly being undermined by her partner. He would deride her in front of friends. They worked in the same company and if they were at a meeting together, he would often demean her contribution. Chris would laugh it off, telling herself that it 'washed over her' and saying that 'he didn't really mean it'. Finally she had had enough and plucked up the courage to leave him, and only then did her friends tell her how embarrassed they had been at his behaviour. She was shocked as she had been in denial as to its severity.

After they separated, they had to work together briefly on a project. He started to undermine her again in front of their colleagues and she was shaking with fury. She took him to one side and asked him never to speak to her like that again. He was dumbfounded. She realised with sudden insight how deeply negative his behaviour had been towards her and how little she had done to defend herself.

3 **You just get rid of all that pent up emotion. If you are angry, you just let rip. It's over in minutes and you feel so much better afterwards.**

There are some people who use emotion as a way of getting rid of tension. If that is carried out on the football pitch or with a box of Kleenex at a sad movie, all is well. However, if the emotion tends to express itself in violence, rages or behind-the-scenes manipulation, then it can damage relationships irretrievably. You may feel better, but what does it leave in its wake?

Jenny was a very bright young woman but when it came to relationships, people were scared of her. If anyone disagreed with her or crossed her in any way her first reaction was belligerence, or a more formal litigious letter from her lawyer would arrive on their doorstep. Being her friend was a trial by fire and many did not last the course. She would always claim she was right, and nobody would deny that, as she was very well versed in all she undertook. However, her anger meant she made so many enemies that she lost out in the long run. She could never understand why people ignored her and her friendships were short lived.

4 **When you feel strong emotion, you know you must act on it. I ignore it at my peril as it is always a sign that things are not right and I must change my circumstances.**

This last approach is really the one we must all adopt. Emotions cannot be run away from, as they do not disappear. You might think they have but they come flooding back, often at quite inappropriate moments.

When I worked in the field of trauma counselling, people would often try to deny the existence of post-traumatic stress disorder, pointing out that many wars have been fought without complaints of this syndrome. For a start these combatants had nothing to call it and no-one to take their problems seriously. But, believe me, they suffered all the symptoms.

A friend of mine recently talked about her 85-year-old grandfather who at Christmas the previous year, started to cry about his war experiences and couldn't stop after seeing a programme on television. He had tried to submerge the images and emotions they engendered to protect his family from the evil they represented. However, they were still there. He had not exorcised those ghosts by not talking about them and by putting his experiences into perspective.

You do not need these unusual, traumatic experiences to have lingering emotions. It could the break up of a relationship, the loss of a job, or the death of a friend or relation. To keep that emotion inside can lead to ulcers and cancers, and to scream and shout can lead to coronary heart disease – and of course becoming a social pariah. (Do read *The Sickening Mind* by Paul Martin for more information on this.) So we must follow another route.

FIVE STEPS TO EMOTIONAL EXPERTISE
Step 1: Know What You are Feeling

It is helpful to be able to name your emotions. Are you wild with rage or mildly irritated? Are you filled with love and happiness or having a rather good time?

I find it really helpful to rate the intensity of the emotion I am expressing on a scale of 1 to 10. It has the immediate effect of lessening the upset and gives me a sense of being in control. This process is, of course, for the negative, uncomfortable emotions of anger and upset. If I am wildly happy I just go with the flow.

Begin to accept emotions for what they are. Do not try to wish them away. You cannot deny yourself or anyone else their right to feel anything – they just do.

So it is a waste of time to think that an emotion is 'wrong'. Just concentrate on feeling it.

Step 2: Read the Emotional Message

If your current relationship makes you feel 'hemmed in', ask yourself why. Work out when you feel this way and what would solve it.

If you are upset or angry after a meeting, it is worth asking other witnesses what they thought. In other words, indulge in some balanced thinking. You may have misread the signals so you might want to reduce seething anger to mild irritation.

A young woman I was coaching told me she was very lonely. She lived with her parents and rarely socialised. Had she always been like this? Apparently not. She said that she had always been the organiser in her social group. One day, she wondered what would happen if she did not phone round her friends. Would they take the initiative? Well they didn't and she then didn't. Her interpretation was that they didn't care enough about meeting up with her. Some of her friends married and she became the hermit she was when I met her.

I asked if her friends met without her. She thought not. So why did she take their absence personally? In fact, they were just disorganised and looked to her to galvanise them into action. When she left my office, she was kicking herself for all the time she had wasted being upset and depressed. She had misinterpreted the situation and her emotion.

But what was great was that she used her loneliness to seek me out. She used the message from that emotion to take action.

Step 3: Use Past Successes

One of the best ways I have found to help me move on from really upsetting emotional situations is to ask myself:

◆ When have I had this feeling before?

◆ How successfully did I cope?

◆ How do I feel now?

Generally, things pass. We cope and we move on. It is rarely the big deal we are making it out to be.

If you remember a time when you were depressed, you probably decided to talk to a close friend, go out for a drink or to a fun movie. And it worked. If you do the same again the chances are that it will work again. The more coping strategies you have, the more you will keep your life on an even keel.

Step 4: Take Action

Uncomfortable emotions like hurt, fear, anger, irritation, guilt, anxiety and abandonment are there for a reason. They are telling you that things are not right and that you must listen to these messages and take appropriate action.

The sooner you take action, the more control you have of your emotions. You will nip depression in the bud while it is still a slight hurt; you will be irritated, not incandescent with rage.

A few years ago, I experienced uncomfortable emotions in a meeting. When the company chairman talked of changes he wanted to make to a project I was heading up, I started to feel cornered and claustrophobic. No more than that. But as I listened, I realised the feeling was becoming stronger. He was trying to remove areas of my responsibility without saying so in a straightforward way. He also wanted to sack staff who were intrinsic to the project's success. Despite remonstrations, the decision stood and I realised there would be no betterment or solution. I became angry and, after consulting friends and advisers, I resigned my position. That powerful feeling of discomfort, of being propelled away from what I believed to be right, helped guide my actions.

Step 5: Focus on Positive Emotions

Emotions that propel you forward in life, that motivate and cultivate, can replace those of negativity. If you fill your life with these, there is less room for the bad ones.

Love, reward, stimulation, enthusiasm, involvement, energy and commitment are all powerful emotions. If you don't feel these often enough, you must change your life to acquire them. Don't wait till you get enough money or the right job partner or even children – do it now.

ACTION

This section looks at how you can change the way you behave and how people respond to you.

BODY LANGUAGE TRICKS

It is worth remembering that you do not need to be confident to start using confident body language. As soon as you straighten your back and look directly at the person you are talking to, you will instantly look more confident. Smiling is the big one. If you have a relaxed smile on your face, you will always be assessed as confident.

BASIC TRICKS

◆ Smile. It changes the chemistry of the body, releasing endorphins to the brain to provide the energy and dynamism associated with confidence.

◆ Walk tall. Your actual height is unimportant.

◆ Look everyone in the eye. Listen intently and nod when in agreement.

◆ Uncross your arms. Crossed arms tend to look closed and unwelcoming. Use gestures that open your body up. This encourages people to talk to you.

◆ Shake hands when you meet people for the first time. This may seem formal but that contact relaxes and bonds. Shake hands when you part and, if the encounter went especially well, add your other hand to their wrist. That gesture really captivates, but only works with sincerity.

◆ Avoid touching your face when speaking. It makes you look ill at ease and anxious.

◆ If you want to appear really absorbed by your partner, you must stare into the other person's eyes, put your hand under your chin and support your elbow with your other arm.

◆ If you want to look relaxed and confident, lean your elbow up against a piece of furniture and perch on the back of a chair or the corner of a table.

◆ Then smile some more.

Every time you walk through a door, straighten your back, look ahead and smile. You never know who might be on the other side. If you are looking at the floor, you might miss an exciting friendship opportunity. Use the door as a trigger, a reminder for a confident posture. Change your body language for THREE weeks then another NINE will turn it into a habit. You do not have to think consciously about it after that: it will be automatic. Such is the nature of learning.

That reminds me of a joke I was told prior to giving a speech to a conference of accountants. I was dared to tell it to them, so of course I did.

How can you tell when an accountant is excited?
He is looking at your feet, not his own.

They all laughed, though what a sad indictment of the profession in terms of public perception.

INSTANT CONFIDENCE TRICKS

Smiling	Happy, confident, at ease
Direct gaze	Nothing to hide, confident in relationships
Head erect, good posture	High self-esteem
Open gestures	Open, honest person
Head to one side	Listening positively
Leaning forward	Interested in what is being said
Nodding	Approval of another person's point of view

PERSONAL APPEARANCE

Appearance is important. If you feel good about how you look, you will automatically be more confident.

I remember seeing on video the famous management guru Tom Peters speak at a toastmasters' awards ceremony where he was voted Speaker of the Year. He cleverly challenged their ten commandmments for giving a good speech, and the bit that stuck in my mind was when he talked about appearance.

He claimed that contrary to their precepts of wearing an expensive well-fitting suit for a presentation, he only had one, which he had been wearing for the past twenty-five years. It fitted him when he was thin and didn't when he put on weight. Of course the toastmasters could hardly assert themselves as they had voted him Speaker of the Year. It was a brilliant side-swipe at their conventional wisdom.

However, we are for the most part less famous than Tom Peters and adhering to some appearance guidelines can help us make an impact when it is necessary. For men, buying at least one good suit for weddings, funerals and that all important interview is essential. A more expensive suit will crumple less and will survive travel and other exigencies.

Like it or not, others do judge us on our appearance and whether 'we look the part' for a particular job. I was coaching a manager for a directorial position with a large insurance company. They described him as 'scruffy'. He had longish hair which hung over his collar and he looked crumpled in his worn suit. He was far from being sartorially elegant. After my hairdresser cut his hair we looked at suits more expensive than he normally bought. He decided not to invest in his appearance and spent the money instead on a holiday. A suit in that league would be bought when he made director. He failed to impress at his interview due in part to his appearance.

For women a good jacket is an essential, especially at work. You can get away with inexpensive skirts, trousers and shirts but a stylish well cut jacket wins the day. Wearing a jacket rather than just a shirt or jumper has been shown by psychologists to imbue the wearer with power, influence and credibility.

I was surprised during my last visit to GMTV to hear that the female presenters bought their tops and tights from Top Shop. They had to wear different outfits every day, which took its toll financially so they wanted value for money and the latest fashion.

The major ingredient of appearance for me has little to do with fashion and much more to do with enthusiasm and energy. If you show that you are excited about your life, your work or your friendships, you will be forgiven for most style offences.

Colour analysts tell us it is the colour we wear round our necks which is important if we want to come across as healthy and confident, not pale and wan. This colour reflects onto our faces and creates a brightness or a sallowness of complexion. For men it means choosing the shirt and tie that suits you; for women the correct colour of jumper, blouse or scarf.

CONFIDENCE MAKEOVER

◆ Stop wearing clothes that you dislike, bought for you as presents by others. Family and friends buy their colours not yours.

◆ Start wearing clothes you have purchased yourself and that make you feel good.

◆ Stop buying bland.

◆ Start buying bright.

◆ Stop just buying for style.

◆ Start buying for colour.

BECOME AN INSIDE-OUT PERSON

The best action confidence trick I know is to become an inside-out person. Of course, the opposite is an outside-in person and I want to describe them first.

They are so focused on their own problems and anxieties that they have no time for anyone else. For the most part, they don't mean to be like this, but their lack of confidence has made them self-obsessed. As they walk into a room it is all about how embarrassed they feel; they don't realise that most people there who are strangers feel just the same. They may even enter the 'but I am worse than you' competition.

Stop right now and start becoming an inside-out person. This is what to do.

◆ Make it your mission to put other people at their ease. Notice when they are looking anxious; look at body language; be aware of whether their tone of voice is relaxed or pitched a little too high.

◆ Get them to talk by asking questions. Open-ended ones are best as they get them talking and then all you have to do is listen.

◆ Use something I call conversational cement. Reward what they are saying to you with 'that's interesting', 'tell me more about that', 'I'm fascinated'. Do not simply rush to what you are going to say next.

◆ Contribute to the conversation with some disclosures of your own. These will encourage the other person.

◆ Seek out common interests or similarities in background. We relax much more with people when we build bridges of experience.

◆ Face them straight on so that you can see their reaction while you are talking. Smile encouragement to put them at their ease.

◆ Practise this as often as possible when you meet other

people for the first time. You will then have no time to worry about your own lack of confidence and, as a result, you will be more confident yourself.

Actions speak louder than words, an old but true adage. Just go out and do it. Then start to join societies or clubs where you get to meet others.

The self-absorption that goes hand in hand with low levels of confidence does not help. Put becoming an inside-out person high on your list of personal confidence tricks.

TEN-SECOND CONFIDENCE TRICKS

◆ As soon as you feel depressed or assailed by negative thoughts, get active. Walk, talk, read or write. Outlaw staring at walls for any longer than one hour. Set your alarm. You are in control of your thoughts.

◆ If upset or angry, ask yourself how strongly you feel on a scale of 1 to 10? This distances you from the emotion and helps you get some rational control.

◆ Put 'your' time in your diary. Say no to anything that encroaches.

◆ When entering a room full of strangers, pause in the doorway, imagining you are your favourite film star. Take on their pose and look around the room to select who, as a star, you would wish to talk to.

> ◆ Faced with a problem or a crisis ask yourself
> how you have coped before and tell yourself 'I
> will cope again'.
>
> ◆ Find something to smile about every day and
> tomorrow will be even better.

Now write your **confidence boosting action plan** as you
review the chapter for the tricks that will help you.

2

CONFIDENCE
WITH LOVERS&PARTNERS

The sweep of this chapter is broad. We will talk about all aspects of the close relationship: how to find one, keep one and cope with one that is fraying at the edges, and what to do if it ends.

Let's start with a reality check of your current situation. Again, there are no right or wrong answers, and this is for your eyes only. If you do not have a partner at present, answer the first four questions.

REALITY-CHECK YOUR CLOSE RELATIONSHIPS

1. Is having a regular lover or partner necessary for maintaining your confidence? ....
Why?...

2. How good are you at being on your own between relationships? ....

3. How good are you at meeting potential partners? ....

4. How good are you at going on first dates? ....

5. Are you committed to your current long-term relationship? ....

6. Does your current partner meet your expectations? ....

7. Do you meet theirs? ....

8. Is your relationship an equal partnership in terms of division of labour at home? ....

9. Is your sex life satisfactory? ....
If not, why not? ....

10. Do you often have fantasies about others? ....

11. Do you act on these fantasies? ....

12. Do you feel guilty about these relationships? ....

13. Do you ever talk to your partner about these fantasies? ....
If not, why not? ....

14. Do you ever talk about shortcomings in the relationship?...
If not, why not? ....

15. Do you feel genuinely loved by your partner?....

16. How often do you tell them how much you love them? ....

17. Would you be frightened to leave this relationship?...
If so, why? ....

18. How well would you cope if it ended? ....

RATING YOUR ANSWERS
Questions 1 to 4

If you answered yes to 1, it is worth thinking about the wisdom of living your life through others, relying on them for the confidence you lack. But what happens if they are suddenly not there? A relationship is a precarious foundation on which to base your life. Better to seek to become a confident person in your own right; then a partner adds value, rather than being a necessity for survival.

Meeting people for dates can be a challenge after college or university years have passed. Getting out there and having the skills to chat, never mind chat up, is essential.

Questions 5 to 8

If you answered negatively to these questions, you could end up in a long-term relationship without really thinking of the implications. Are you committed or are you filling in between more exciting opportunities? If the latter applies, you might be better on your own.

Martyrdom in a relationship is not healthy. Start as you mean to continue and negotiate an equal distribution of tasks. It is much more difficult to change habits once they become established.

If you answered no to any of these questions, start reviewing your partnership and draw up a survival plan.

Questions 9 to 14

Sex turns a friendship into a close relationship. But just like everything else, you have to negotiate what each of you wants. Having fantasies about others is normal but can point to something lacking in your current relationship. Guilt will just compound the problem; lying increases stress and shortens your life.

If you do not tell your partner about your fantasies, how can they know what you like – telepathy? Unless you can talk about shortcomings, they will become destructive. As soon as you act on your fantasies about other people, you will detract from your current partnership.

Count up your 'no' answers for this section and add these to your list of goals.

Questions 15 to 18

Loving openly and being loved is the purpose of an intimate relationship. Anything less than that should be discussed. Also, if you are worried about your survival if a relationship ended, challenge that realistically. There is nothing worse than staying with a bad relationship for fear of being on your own.

Review your answers for this section and add them to your goal list.

FORMING RELATIONSHIPS

Despite more openness about sex and a greater equality in roles taken by the sexes, relationships do not seem to have become any easier. I read an article about the novelist Beryl Bainbridge, who is now in her 60s. She recounted that she used to go out with men she only quite liked because it was the polite thing to do. Men, I am sure you cannot rely on that nowadays.

So relationship forming is risky. Risky in case your overtures are rejected, risky because of all the ramifications of emotional involvement and investment. But worth the risk surely?

I am always fascinated by what brings people together. Here is a synopsis of research into how relationships come about by academic psychologists Munton, Silvester, Stratton and Hanks, entitled 'Attributions in Action'.

HOW RELATIONSHIPS COME ABOUT – THE BASIC REQUIREMENTS

Attractive and accessible. The first is obvious but the second in this e-mail day and age might be challenged. Still, e-mail is accessibility, I suppose. I remember a survey some years ago published by Mills & Boon, which revealed that proximity was a major criterion for men when choosing a mate. That is why so many doctors choose to marry nurses, directors their secretaries and so on. For women, the choice was found to be more complex and had to do with attraction and friendship.

So in marketing terms the goods need to be well packaged and available for consumption!

Appropriateness. For a relationship to work, each must feel the other to be at the same or a similar level so that one is not wildly more advantaged than the other.

Matching needs. If one member of a couple wants a close relationship while the other just wants a fling, the union is destined for a swift conclusion.

Partner provides interesting differences. The old adage of opposites attracting seems to be borne out in research. Why spend time with someone exactly the same as ourselves?

Mutual influencing. There is an expectation that each member of the couple is influencing the other in some kind of way, that they are responsive to the other's needs. You certainly notice where that is not happening when relationships go sour. Then quite the opposite occurs. A relationship often goes wrong when one person stops learning from the other.

So how do you meet someone to start all this mutual influencing? For those of you already in a relationship, skip to the next section, but keep reading if you are between lovers.

DATING CONFIDENCE

There are so many tricks attached to dating, many of which are to be seen in reality TV programmes. So let's look at some of the basic ones.

◆ **GO OUT.** There is no use complaining that you cannot find a date if you do not go to places where dates can be found. I was recently coaching a young woman to increase her confidence. She had got into the habit of staying at home during the weekend with her parents. Her girlfriends were all married and beginning to produce babies so she felt like the only one left on the shelf. A previous relationship had failed and she had lost confidence socially. She would be invited to a party, accept and then not turn up. The first goal she had to achieve was to phone her remaining single friends and make arrangements for the weekend in a place where dates might be found. The opposite sex are not going to beat a path to your door, especially if they never see you. Also, the more you go out, the less of a big deal it is.

◆ **GO TO THE RIGHT PLACES.** Before embarking on the dating game you must first work out what your target market is. If you want to date an artist, steer clear of a haunt frequented by investment bankers. Also, take age range into consideration. If you want a more mature relationship eschew the student pub in favour of the upmarket hotel bar.

◆ **DO NOT HUNT IN PACKS.** There may be safety in numbers but how can a woman make your acquaintance if you are in a gang of drinking buddies? And it is just too difficult for a guy to run the verbal gamut of a gaggle of women. He will go for an easier target. Do not misunderstand me – going out with a group can be great fun but do not expect it to lead to a date. One or two friends would be better than a group.

Even more successful would be going out or travelling by yourself. It is by far the best way to meet people. I went on holiday by myself for the first time last year. I had always travelled abroad on business or to speak at conferences by myself but not on holiday. I have to say it was a great experience. Hotels and restaurants find it strange for a woman to be on her own but do not be put off by that. People were only too delighted to chat and include me in their group.

◆ **MAKE FRIENDS.** Rather than building dating into a 'big thing', set out to make friendships. I know this strategy may be anathema to men, especially as your focus is primarily on sex as the ultimate goal, but believe me – making friends with women will work for them. And call me a pragmatic Scot but I would always do what works. Chat-up lines massacred by guys and flicky eyelash and touching routines favoured by women are all a bit transparent.

Just be interested, ask questions, listen and talk. If you are wondering what to ask, there is a formula that allows you to get to know anyone, even if you have only five minutes waiting in a queue. It is called F.O.R.E.

F.O.R.E.

F AMILY
O CCUPATION
R ECREATION
E DUCATION

If you ask questions in the above areas you will get to know someone very quickly. You do not need chat-up lines to impress with your wit and repartee. What you are doing is finding out if you have common interests, views about life, backgrounds and aspirations. You can then progress to discover more, hand him or her on to a friend or move on to another person you find interesting.

If you really want someone to warm to you, smile and compliment them. I don't mean in a sycophantic or sleazy way but reward them for a unique or particular quality that appeals to you. I saw the power of this in action one year on holiday in Lanzarote. Two guys were in the apartment next to us. While Mike was quiet Bill was quite the opposite. At night in the bar, Bill was always surrounded by beautiful girls. He wasn't particularly handsome. In fact, Mike, the quiet one, was probably the better looking of the duo. But Bill was captivating, and I was dying to know the secret of his success – just so I could write about it in a book of course!

One evening we walked down the street to the bar with him. It took some time as he would stop a girl in the street and compliment her on her outfit, her hair, her smile – whatever captivated him at the time. The compliments were genuinely given. He would then ask her to accompany him to the bar, promising her a fun evening. It was like being with the Pied Piper. Our small group grew as all these women joined us to go to the bar. And it was a fun evening as he chatted to these young women in turn. He brought the best out in them by being such rewarding company. He did not make the mistake that most men do of showing off and talking too much about himself. He talked briefly and listened a lot. Always positive, always complimentary. The women loved him.

The girl he chose to date for the rest of the holiday was a young woman on the periphery of the group who was quieter but intelligent and charming. He was good at choosing some-one who would complement him.

I can hear the cynics among you saying that he had the charm, it was easy for him. But these skills are not unattain-able. Let's list what they are so that you can practise. And this is not a sex-specific thing. I may have given an example of a captivating man but women can try this too – it works just as well with men.

> # THE SKILLS
>
> **Smile**
>
> **Compliment genuinely**
>
> **Ask questions**
>
> **Listen**
>
> **Compliment more**

◆ **DON'T PUT ALL YOUR EGGS...** Do not rely on one encounter during an evening or even one fancied person. Spread your friendships more widely and date a few people. Practise – it makes for perfection.

◆ **MARKET YOURSELF WELL** Aim to look good, the best you can be. If that means getting a good haircut, buying a new shirt or wearing your favourite outfit, put yourself out a bit. All the dating makeover programmes you see on television don't spend time on how people look for nothing. We should all know by now that it takes about five seconds to make a bad first impression and about thirty to make a good one.

FIRST DATE TRICKS

If all your marketing has worked and you are preparing for the first date, here are some first date tricks that will have you ready for love.

BE BUSY

Do not be so anxious about this date that you become obsessed by it. Keep busy doing other things. Perhaps line up other dates so that you are completely relaxed about this special one.

BE INTERESTED

If this is going to be more than a one-night stand, you must get to know this potential partner as much as possible. To keep the conversation flowing, ask the right questions. I am not talking about content, more about the style of asking. If you ask open-ended rather than closed questions, your date will relax and open up to you. A list of types of question is below. In the main, what you are trying to avoid is asking questions that can be answered by 'yes' or 'no', the reason being that you will get through a heap of questions and your conversation will sound like an interrogation.

TYPES OF QUESTIONS

CLOSED	OPEN	PROBING
Are?	What?	How?
Do?	Which?	In what way?
Have?	Where?	Tell me more
	Who?	Describe in more detail
	Why?	For what reasons?

You will notice that probing questions have been added to the list. If you really want to get to know someone quickly but in depth, try these for size. By asking probing questions you get behind the glib reply and the ready answer.

BE BOLD

Respond with bold enthusiasm to your date. If you like them, show that you do. The kind of insouciant game-playing that has you looking so cool you are frosty is too exhausting and ends up giving the message that you don't care.

BE SOBER

It is a bad idea to get so drunk that you feel no pain. You may be oblivious but your date isn't. And they are less likely to want to repeat the process on another occasion. If you don't care, drunkenness may help to pass the evening but if you do care, stay sober.

BE RELAXED

There is a great mind game for a first date. When you wake in the morning and you are still in that lovely warm, emergent state, imagine your date as clearly as you can – meeting, chatting, walking, eating or watching a movie. Visualise looking into their eyes and them yours. You are like a magnet attracting them with your gaze and your warmth. Then tell yourself that this is how it is going to be.

ARE YOU DOWN DATING?

Perhaps you are way beyond the first date and wondering if this person is the partner for you. It is so easy to get into the habit of having a relationship around. It makes life easier. So often there is a reluctance to take a cool look at our partner in case we don't like what we see. The implications are disruptive but better earlier on before the commitment to a marriage or a mortgage.

I have drawn up a questionnaire for you to test your relationship and answer the question, are you 'down dating'? Are you having a relationship with someone who is not a match for you, is not pulling their weight or is not treating you in the way that you deserve?

See how you get on and worry about what you need to do to get back on track later.

ARE YOU WITH THE RIGHT PARTNER?

1. When someone comes over to talk to you in a bar do you think...

a) they work in the bar?

b) they fancy your friend?

c) they fancy you?

2. When close friends ask you and your partner to dinner, do you...

a) say 'some time soon, when the time is right'?
b) avoid the situation – they will not get on with your partner?
c) accept immediately – it will be great for everyone to get to know each other?

3. It's your birthday. Your partner turns up looking scruffy. They haven't bothered to change to take you out. Do you...
a) tell them that they could have tried harder?
b) accept them as they are – after all, who are you to judge?
c) suggest that they change? It is a special night.

4. You come back to your flat after a night out. Your partner has been watching TV all evening but has not cleared up and the flat is a mess. Do you...
a) tell your partner, as you always do, that their behaviour is not good enough?
b) clear up yourself, as you always do?
c) remind them of what you agreed and give them an ultimatum to change?

RESULTS

If you scored four Cs or a majority of Cs, you are not down dating. You have good self-esteem and rate your partner highly. You are also assertive and able to deal with your partner if they are in any way disrespectful.

If you scored four As or a majority of As, you are indulging in avoidance. Your self-esteem could be higher and although you might be unhappy, you are not confronting issues. You need to discuss the relationship to see where it is going and take remedial action.

If you scored four Bs or a majority of Bs, you are down dating. You are accepting a level of relationship that is poor and is probably undermining your already shaky self-esteem. You really know that you need to move on but you may fear that you might not find another relationship easily. You could start with simple confidence boosters such as expanding your social life, or getting a new look, haircut or clothes. Even more important, however, is believing that you are worth it.

KNOWING WHEN A RELATIONSHIP IS RIGHT

How can you be confident that a particular relationship is a special one, the one that is going to last? Life moves so fast and circumstances fluctuate with increasing speed. In that maelstrom, can we tell which of our partnerships will have longevity?

Many of my friends have had long, close relationships, and I have made a study of the elements that distinguish them from their more ephemeral counterparts. The results are contained in the questionnaire below. Answer the questions honestly and you will gain insight into whether your current relationship will stand the test of time.

THE EMOTIONAL COMMITMENT SCALE

1. When you first met, did you feel exhilarated?
2. Does your partner bring out the best in you?
3. When they enter a room, does it light up for you?
4. Do you see the world from a different perspective through their eyes?
5. Do you enjoy just doing nothing together?
6. Do you have interests in common?
7. If your partner went on holiday without you, would you trust them implicitly?
8. Can you settle differences swiftly, coming up with solutions that work?
9. Do you complement each other with different skills?
10. Do you work together on domestic projects with a fair division of labour?
11. Is your sexual relationship experimental and exciting?
12. Do you talk about each other to friends using positive and enthusiastic language?
13. Are the friends that matter comfortable with you both as a couple?
14. Do you find it difficult to imagine life without them?

There is a mixture of attributes in this list. Do you need to have all of the ingredients? The majority, yes. If there is a lack in one area, that tends to become exaggerated over time rather than improving. If, for example, you do not trust your partner, getting married to them is not going to alleviate that fear. A marriage certificate will not bind this person to you.

It is certainly worthwhile discussing these points and negotiating changes before marriage or moving in together. It would seem that you lose some valuable leverage once you commit yourself to the relationship in a more formal way.

People often use marriage as a tool for change whereas the opposite is true. Once married, both parties tend to become more entrenched, not less so.

A colleague of mine discovered that her boyfriend had continued to see an old flame throughout their relationship. She was understandably very upset, and he suitably repentant. He suggested that marriage would solve his philandering behaviour and she felt that this might represent new beginnings in their relationship.

Now, some 10 years on, she knows that he has always had relationships on the side. And only recently did she discover that he had been in contact – and she has still to discover what kind of contact – with that old flame.

People do change and a close relationship has turned around many a person, but you have to be very sure that your chosen partner buys into what you have negotiated. And you must give them time to prove themselves. Do not do as many have done and jump in on a wing and a prayer.

MEN, WOMEN AND RELATIONSHIPS

Talking of negotiating, many partnerships split up because one or both parties do not know how to influence the other. It is here that sex differences are most apparent. There are some basic principles that are worth remembering.

SIMPLE SEX PRINCIPLES

Men like to sort stuff out and be heroes and women like to care and nurture.

Men are drawn to things and tasks, women to people.

Women problem solve by talking, men by themselves.

Women multi-task, men focus.

Research psychologists now say that in the nature–nurture debate nature is winning. So forget political correctness – we are different. That does not mean, however, that both sexes should not have equality of opportunity or parity of wage. We are just different.

So the sex principles affect how we must influence the opposite sex. There is nothing more boosting to confidence than discovering that you have influenced successfully. So let's start with how women should negotiate with men.

INFLUENCING TRICKS FOR WOMEN
1: Let Them Slay Dragons for You

Sunny Crouch, who set up the World Trade Centre in London, spoke at a 'Women in Business' conference recently. Her advice to those assembled was about how to get the support of your partner if you are planning to set up a business of your own. You will need that support, so do not alienate those nearest and dearest to you. She, like me, was writing a book, and her husband had been complaining that he never saw her when she returned home from London at the weekend.

This particular weekend, she had agreed to go shopping for garden equipment but she was behind her deadline for submitting her book. Now, she could have asserted herself and told him how important this deadline was. She could have stayed in London and avoided the confrontation. What she did do was ask for his help with the dilemma. She had given her word about the garden trip but she had this deadline. He suggested that he go himself and phone her from the centre for her instructions. Then she could get on with her book as she honoured her commitment. He felt happy that he had solved her problem and been the hero with the equipment. He even made supper so that she could finish her book!

So ask for help and then run with whatever they suggest. That way every one wins. A good relationship fosters confidence; a limiting one undermines.

2: Avoid the Telepathy Trap

Remember that men are very focused on what they are doing. Do not expect them to pick up on subtleties or martyrdom. Nods, winks and body language pass them by and banged doors are surely just caused by the wind. So when you want something, be clear and exact.

Do not expect them to know telepathically what you would like for your birthday, for example. There is no use complaining after the event when you have been given chocolates once again when you would have loved a bunch of flowers. 'Surely he knew I was on a diet,' you may cry. The answer is probably not, since he has always liked you the way you are, not a slimmer version.

Just ask for flowers.

3: Timing is Everything

Men like to focus on one thing at a time so you must choose your moment to have that important conversation. If he is watching television, do not expect to have even a semblance of a conversation because he won't remember a word of it. He is so focused on whatever the programme has to offer that you will be a mere buzz of interference on the periphery of his concentration.

There is no use being offended by this. It is how men for the most part are. So choose your moment with care – one when you will have his undivided attention.

4: Don't Nag, Negotiate

Do what works. Clearly nagging does not work for, by its very definition, it is continuous. It is also exhausting if you are the nagger.

Everything in life is a negotiation, sometimes perhaps even a compromise. So if you want something carried out in the house, negotiate what he could get in return for his participation. Understand his point of view first, then let him understand yours. Then you can discuss a solution. Perhaps he does not want to get stuck into the DIY as soon as he comes home. Perhaps he could read the paper first then get started.

But, I hear you cry, he never does get started. Then you don't cook supper for him, if that was part of the negotiation. If, for example, you cook dinner and your partner's part of the bargain is to clear and wash up afterwards, then do not under any circumstances do it all yourself. If he fails to do his share, leave the table and the dishes till the next evening if you have to.

Where we, as women, tend to go wrong is that we capitulate, carrying out our side of the bargain anyway because someone has to, and it is usually us. Do not give in to that. It means that you have no leverage to get compliance from him. If the guidelines are there, follow them consistently or he will know he can get away with murder.

INFLUENCING TRICKS FOR MEN
1: Listen

Women talk about issues and problems before coming to conclusions. They do not really want decisions made for them or even suggestions as to the best solutions. They just want a sounding board. So when men offer 10 sterling solutions to resolve their difficulties they can feel thoroughly rebuffed when these are discarded without due care and attention.

There is no use being upset about this. It is just how women are.

She would love you, however, to listen as she tells you her troubles. A glass of wine, a shoulder massage and a footstool are optional extras if you want to go for advanced influencing. When she has come up with her solutions, that is the time to add in a few of your own, or helpful modifications. But only after you have heard hers.

2: A Hug Works

When women are upset and angry, as you are listening try a hug as well.

When I was vexed by something that happened with a client I remember stating very clearly to my partner that I would really like a hug.

His reply was that it was difficult trying to hug a porcupine. So no matter how bristly we might appear, hug us anyway. We will be putty in your hands.

3: Stick to Promises

Women are a little like elephants – they tend not to forget. So if you promise to do something, no matter how insignificant it may be to you, your partner will be waiting for some action. If you forget, it will be labelled as not caring. So do not make promises lightly, and be prepared to carry them out.

4: Talk

Even if your partner is busy doing the multi-tasking thing women do so well, do talk to her. It may look as if she is totally involved in work or family, but she can also cope with you talking to her.

A big mistake men make is believing that because there are problems elsewhere in the family, at work or financially, women will not want to be bothered by any additional angst that their man might have. Angst is what women are good at and the way you will influence us is to open up. Women do not need you to be a hero all the time. A partner who loves you will love you even more for your vulnerability.

For the last three years, a male friend has been wrestling to regain control of his company. He gave away his shareholding in exchange for an investment he dearly needed. However, the investors ganged up against him and he lost his controlling interest, and therefore his independence. You only had to look at him to see the strain. He sought legal redress and recently won his action. I asked how his wife was feeling now that the day had been saved. He told me that he had not involved his wife because she was going through a lot of change and stress at work. If I had been her, I would have been furious.

A relationship is for sharing the bad times as well as the good. I am sure she would rather have known about the difficulties he was facing. Women usually know instinctively when something is wrong. Men, you must realise that a woman will normally think the problem lies with her until you tell her otherwise. So if you want to influence us, understand that we like to get to the heart of the matter. Confide in us. Caring is what we do well.

The relatively high rates of depression and suicide among men may be related to the fact that they keep so much to themselves.

RELATIONSHIP ROT

Even with all the hope and commitment in the world, some relationships will not make it. And sometimes we let a poor and fading relationship continue well past its sell-by date. Don't get me wrong – I think you must try everything to make a relationship work, especially if you have invested time and effort in it.

If confidence in your relationship has plummeted, it helps to notice the signs of relationship rot as soon as possible so that you can take evasive action. Use the following to review your current partnership.

RATING YOUR RELATIONSHIP ROT

1. Do you go out to the cinema or for a meal less often than you used to?

2. Do you celebrate special occasions less often than you used to?

3. Does your partner tend to put you down in front of their friends?

4. Do you put your partner down in front of your friends?

5. Do you just eat in front of the television now rather than laying the table for dinner?

6. Do you both eye up other talent when you go out together?

7. Do you both read in bed now more than you make love?

8. Has lovemaking become, frankly, just a bit boring?

9. Are the presents you give each other now more practical than sexy or fun?

10. Do you feel that you are both stuck in a rut?

Now, you must realise that each question taken individually may not mean anything much at all. But if you are answering yes to more than two or three questions, it is time for a chat.

If you have hit the jackpot with ten yes answers, your relationship is in need of an emergency overhaul.

Rating your relationship rot is a great reality check, so do not be depressed by the results. It is a little like experiencing the uncomfortable emotions we talked about in Chapter 1. (And you may in fact be experiencing an uncomfortable emotion right now as you contemplate your options.) This is not a bad thing as it can spur you to take action to do everything to salvage your relationship or move on with your life.

Below are some suggestions for stimulating your relationship. Try these ideas for one week only and then assess the results. Involve your partner in the process or just try changing yourself. Do what you think is best.

THE KISS-OF-LIFE RELATIONSHIP MAKEOVER

◆ Only say positive things to and about your partner for a week. No put-downs, underminings or teasings.
◆ Remember the attributes that first drew you to your partner. Focus on those when they appear and compliment them. If you reward something you will get more of it. It is a simple psychological rule.
◆ Make a couple of dates in your diary to go out together that week without friends and family.
◆ Take up a common interest or join a club together.
◆ Go shopping together and each buy something to wear that you both like.
◆ Try out some new sexual tricks. Books and videos can help.
◆ Have dinner together at home at the dining table and add some candles. Take turns to cook.
◆ Buy something silly for your partner at the end of the week.

◆ Review how the week has gone and how you feel. Has the kiss of life worked on your relationship? If not, why not? If there are signs of life, do you want to continue with the makeover? If so, just do more of the above. More diary dates, shared interests, romantic dinners, bedtime tricks.

If, sadly, you decide that the relationship is dead or that your partner is simply not willing to play, then you must have some difficult conversations. You do not need to feel that this is the end of the world. There is life beyond the relationship. And even here there are some confidence tricks which will help you get over past relationships and prepare for the next.

END-OF-THE-ROAD TRICKS

GRIEVE for the loss of your partner. This is an emotional process which will take a little time. Do not pretend not to care when quite clearly you did and do. There are some things you can do to speed up the process and help you move on, but we are still talking months rather than weeks, depending on the length of your relationship. So don't have unrealistic ideas of recovery.

VISUALISE your ex at their worst – mid-angry outburst, first thing in the morning, whatever it takes. This allows you to withdraw affection. It is the reverse process of when you first met and fell in love. You imagined all their little endearing foibles, sometimes being unable to concentrate on anything else. You are simply turning that process on its head, helping you gain emotional mastery. Sitting around moping, forever mourning the loss of what you had is not propelling you towards your future.

THROW OUT REMINDERS. Gather together photographs, trinkets, clothes, cards, presents you do not want to keep and put them in a large heap. Cut them up and throw them out. This is a kind of ritual cleansing, a symbolic act of termination.

ALLOW ONE MONTH for every year your relationship lasted before you can realistically fall in love again. You can make friendships, date, do what you want to do, but do not expect to feel love for a while. Forcing it will lead you to make mistakes, and words like rebound come to mind.

AVOID going out with just about anything that moves. This shows a quiet desperation. Especially avoid doing a Rod Stewart and picking up a replica of the previous partner. It does not show that you are over anything, more that you are pretending nothing has happened. And that is sad.

TELL YOURSELF that you are merely between partners at the moment and expunge the 'I will never find someone as great again' thoughts. The former is more realistic and keeps you going so that you are still taking care of yourself and not slumping into an alcoholic or carbohydrate stupor.

BE DISCRIMINATING with potential partners. Do not be hysterically grateful that anyone shows an interest in you. Take time to choose.

LOVE LIFE. Enjoy your single status. Do things you have never done before. Do things that perhaps your relationship did not allow you to do. Let your couple friends be jealous of your freedom.

GO FISHING. There are more fish in the sea, so go fishing.

When the time is right you will start dating again, so go back to the beginning of this chapter for those confidence tricks.

TEN-SECOND CONFIDENCE TRICKS

◆ If you are single, research where your target market of men or women go for relaxation.

◆ A recent BBC survey revealed that the majority of relationships outside work started in the gym, so get yourself a membership.

◆ Get into the habit of cultivating the 10-second eye contact gaze for those you fancy.

◆ Go out by yourself sometimes, as you are more likely to meet your mate on your own.

◆ Tell yourself every morning as you look in the mirror that you are worth being dated by an attractive soul mate.

◆ Keep the embers of passion glowing with videos, books and weekends *à deux*.

◆ Talk about how you feel. Don't let resentment build for more than a day.

◆ Concentrate on what you love, not what you hate, in your relationship.

◆ Use a scale of 1 to 10 to assess your confidence in your current relationship. Take action if you rate it below 7.

Now write your **confidence boosting action plan** as you review the chapter for the tricks that will help you.

3

CONFIDENCE
WITH YOUR FAMILY

Families. We all have them in some form or another. How we respond to and interact with our parents will in turn affect how we deal with our own children. And in a cocktail of nature and nurture we will for the most part turn out like our parents.

I remember saying this to a group of lawyers I was teaching at one of my confidence conferences. One of the partners was horrified at the mere mention of such a thing and dismissed my statement out of hand. Most people understand parental influence to be in the content of their lives – what job they have or what house they live in – rather than in the process, such as how they handle relationships. This lawyer had come from a family who were not professionals and who had never attended university, so she saw herself as dramatically different from her background. However, I will bet my life that one or other of her parents was dismissive of arguments and rather belligerent in the face of information they did not want to hear. Just like her.

The way we handle situations, interact with people, think, cope with conflict and deal generally with our emotions will be profoundly influenced by our parents, as they are the first people we encounter when we arrive into the world. We are, of course, sentient human beings and these things are not immutable, but it takes work and persistence to change.

So let's do what we usually do at the beginning of a chapter and get a snapshot of how you interact with your family. Answer the questions below and then we can continue with the substance of this chapter, helping you to increase your levels of confidence with your family – parents, siblings and children.

REALITY-CHECK YOUR FAMILY

1. Do I feel close to my parents? ....
If not, why not? ....

2. Do I still feel criticised by them? ....
If so, why? ....

3. Did I go my own way or did I fulfil their dreams for me?...

4. Did I experience sibling rivalry as a child? ....

5. Do I still keep in contact with my siblings? ....

6. Does the rivalry still exist?......................................

7. Do I let my parents have free access to my children?..
If not, why not?...

8. If they treated my children in a way I disapproved of would I let them know?.....................
If not, why not?...

9. Am I respected by my parents and my children?...
If not, why not?...

10. Do my children help out around the house?......
If not, why not?...

11. Do my children work hard for their pocket money?..
If not, why not?...

12. Am I prepared to deprive them of a treat or their pocket money for wrongdoing?........................
If not, why not?...

13. Do my partner and I show a united front to the children when it comes to matters of discipline?....
If not, why not?...

14. Do I listen to my children?.................................

15. Do I listen to my children when they complain about how they are being treated?...........................
If not, why not? ....

16. Do I treat them all equally, showing no favouritism?...

17. Do I encourage them with praise more than I punish or criticise them? ....

18. Do I take time to discuss and resolve problems with the children ....
If not, why not? ....

19. Do I encourage my children to make independent decisions? ....
If not, why not? ....

20. Am I letting my children go as they grow into young adults?...
If not, why not? ....

RATING YOUR ANSWERS
Questions 1 to 6

If you have answered no to question 1, you may want to contemplate how you could change this situation. Having a close relationship with our parents fosters confidence, as we know we are loved. Getting close if we have not been may take more time and contact.

If you answered yes to 2, you may need to assert yourself about what sort of relationship works for you. Parents will criticise but does it still affect you to the extent that your confidence is undermined or you are deflected from what you want to do?

If you didn't go your own way but pursued parental dreams, re-examine what you want to do and find a way to do it.

If you have experienced sibling rivalry and this continues to haunt you, remind yourself of your strengths and achievements.

Questions 7 to 9

If you answered no to these questions you need to review your interaction with your parents. For a start, you need to be certain that your parents are in agreement with you about how you are bringing up your children.

Asserting yourself with your parents so as not offend but to achieve harmony is important, especially as they will feel they have more experience than you. If you are ignored or disrespected, be prepared to issue house rules or guidelines and stick to your guns.

Questions 10 to 13

If you have answered no to any questions in this section, it is worth rethinking your strategy with your children. They need to learn the rules of good behaviour at home to prepare them for the adult world. And you as a parent need help around the house.

Pocket money should be given as a reward for endeavour not provided as a right. An essential lesson for children to learn is that you are rewarded for good behaviour not bad, and that confidence comes from contribution.

Confidence as a parent comes from knowing that your children are not going to run wild. Confidence as a child comes from the predictability of your parents' behaviour towards you. Inconsistency is undermining and destabilising.

Questions 14 to 18

The questions in this section are difficult to answer honestly. It is probably worth asking your children for feedback. So if you have answered no to any of these questions, rethink your family environment because it may not be conducive to the confidence of your children. They are emerging young adults with distinctive points of view. How will you know what these are if you do not listen or simply reiterate your own? Listening to complaints is more demanding as the temptation to enforce your will is strong.

We are often drawn to the child who reflects our personality so we must make sure each child knows what distinct contribution they bring to the family.

With question 17 the answer is simple: reward motivates, punishment undermines. In question 18 spending time helping your children to problem-solve pays dividends as it will create a sense of mastery, which is so essential to confidence.

Questions 19 and 20

If you answered no to these final questions, then please try to change the situation. Learning independence at an early age prepares children for self-reliance later in life. It is one of life's paradoxes that the more you try to engineer that your children leave home as soon as they are able, the more they wish to stay. Letting go is an important milestone in their lives as well as yours.

The questions above set the agenda for this chapter. How we deal with our parents and our children are connected in ways we may not yet understand. But connected they are. And as we grow older and our children become adults, so our roles change and develop.

THE EIGHT FAMILY MYTHS

So how would you like to increase your levels of confidence with your family? Most parents would settle for knowing that they have done the right thing by their children. Perhaps you would also like to live in a little more peace and harmony; family battles can be so draining. You may want to avoid being embarrassed by your family when you have to go to that more formal occasion. Or you may wish to get a little more support for what you are trying to do in your own life. Whatever the aims you have for this chapter, there are some myths that have to be dispelled. I have called them the eight family myths.

MYTH 1:
There is a state of perfection that can be reached in family life.

You might never make family life perfect, so don't even try. But there are some guidelines that will decrease anxiety and harassment and increase emotional involvement. You will have some of the strengths and weaknesses of your parents, and your children will have some of yours. It is not a perfect world.

MYTH 2:
You should try to give your children all the things you did not get as a child.

Well, it didn't mess you up to get very little as a child, but giving them everything certainly will.

I remember a conference audience being horrified that I applauded a German couple who were millionaires and did not give their children anything they did not work for. They received no pocket money, no treats, no holidays unless they fulfilled their duties around the house. When they were old enough, around six as I remember, they worked in pairs in the family business. Each pair was more successful and earned more than the best salesman working for their parents. There was no enforcement that I could see. They really wanted to prove themselves and earn their way.

Perhaps a little extreme for some, but the principles are there. Giving without earning is a bad idea. For children to understand the value of things they need to have been rewarded for some aspect of good behaviour. It is a great preparation for working life.

MYTH 3:
It is good to be positive all the time with children, telling them how good they are even when they clearly are not.

Encouragement in childhood is essential or children would accomplish less than they should. Blanket approval, however, is unrealistic and leads children to have ridiculous expectations about how life really is. I was speaking to some teachers recently who were having a tricky time helping children come to terms with the fact that they were great at some things and not at others. Their parents had so inflated their egos and skills that the children were divorced from reality. To do this is to misunderstand positive thinking and reward. Criticism delivered in a helpful way, a way that allows children to change their behaviour and come to terms with their weaknesses, is just as positive. Of course, put-downs and attempts to undermine are not.

To give you an example, I wanted to be an opera singer for as long as I can remember. I did get the chance to sing in the chorus of Scottish Opera and had a wonderful time. But sitting at the side of the stage listening to Mirella Freni singing Micaela with Placido Domingo as Don José in *Carmen*, I realised that I could never be that good. Now literature is filled with people persistently plugging away till they reached the hundredth or thousandth rejection and then making it. I think it is just as positive for me to have realised my limitations and then to have focused on other strengths that I had. And so it is with children. Positive thinking of an unrealistic sort can damage.

MYTH 4:
Children are in ever-present danger of being molested by strangers and predators lying in wait for them on the streets.

It is terrifying to hear in the media about the abduction of young children. Of course, all you want to do is draw your offspring to you and never let them out of your sight. However, the statistics do not reveal any increase in this type of crime. The media coverage is so compelling that we imagine it is on the increase but it is not. Teenage crime is; child abduction or molestation is not. And nasty behaviour in the family, although more frequently reported, is probably about the same in terms of incidence. So holding children back from becoming independent is not a good idea.

MYTH 5:
Children should be seen and not heard.

This statement was often repeated in my youth in some kind of vain hope of shutting me up. It clearly never worked. But it always made me wonder why they ever thought it should. Children have acute perceptions of what is going on, some of them breathtakingly accurate and others slightly more askew.

A friend's sister had a second baby recently. They already had a delightful little boy called Richard. When the friend's family were told, her three-year-old daughter instead of being delighted with the new arrival, started crying. In between howls she could just be heard to say, 'But what about Richard?' Clearly, she thought that new babies replaced the previous models. Thank goodness she was heard and seen or nightmares about her own sell-by date would have been on the cards.

In fact, family involvement is key to success. Everyone should have input without parents pulling rank, and with children's suggestions being taken seriously. Helping children to think for themselves and giving them the confidence to speak out is a major parenting skill.

MYTH 6:
Children are really very robust and will bounce back from even the worst situations.

I have spoken at length to child psychologist friends and

colleagues about this and they mostly agree that this is only true if the child's upset is taken seriously and they are provided with the same help and support that any adult would need.

There is an unspoken suggestion in this statement that because children are small and developing then any trauma is less well remembered and more easily assimilated. I do not think there is any evidence to support this. In fact, because the child may not be able to make sense of a situation, it can be even more frightening, and this fear can linger well into adulthood without being understood.

I recall working on the case of a man who was frightened of blood – his own and other people's – and any potentially bloody circumstances. He would faint at anything that even resembled blood. He had no idea why and even felt slightly foolish about his persistent phobia. It had affected his working life. He couldn't drive for fear of fainting and was beginning to be afraid of socialising at all.

When asked about his background, he explained that he had been orphaned at the age of three. He knew nothing of his parents and was told that he had been abandoned. A psychologist colleague decided to explore further and made a trip to the library to look at local newspapers around the time the patient was three years old. What he discovered was that his parents had both been shot by armed robbers in the farm-house where they lived. The child, our client, had hidden under the kitchen table and heard the shooting but had seen nothing of the incident, only his parents' blood as it dripped onto the floor. His aunts, who looked after him, decided not to tell him anything about his parents or the incident in the hope that he would be as robust as they were. They thought 'what he didn't know wouldn't harm him'.

This is an extreme case but the principle remains that children are as affected by trauma and adversity as we are as adults, perhaps more so, as they do not have the advantage of being able to put things into context.

MYTH 7:
Sibling rivalry is motivating and healthy.

As long as there are families, there will be rivalry among brothers and sisters. However, should it be encouraged and fostered, and is it always a good thing?

Comparisons of any kind are usually odious, be they inside or outside the family. They usually mean we are falling short and someone else is better than we are. Of course, that can be motivational as we strive to be equal. However, the prevailing feeling is of being undermined and undervalued. As a psychologist, I uncover examples of sibling rivalry in adults still striving to surpass that elder brother or sister (and they usually are older) instead of celebrating their unique contribution to life.

As parents, you can celebrate and reward the individual capabilities of children. If you do have to treat a child differently from the rest, take time to explain why. Paranoia abounds when there is an absence of information.

MYTH 8:
Cutting yourself and your family off from your own parents will stop past influences affecting you.

Your parents' influence is alive and well within you whether or not you ever see them again. As an adult, it is far better to work through any anger or frustration you may have about your upbringing instead of shutting it out. I am a firm believer that if you have the chance to assert your independence with your parents, you can tackle anyone or anything, especially your own relationships and children.

I was coaching a very pleasant man who was a senior director for a manufacturing company. He had to travel the world setting up new businesses and was held in high regard in this global organisation. However, those more senior to him felt he lacked something – assertiveness, presence, oomph. They struggled to find the right description. Suffice it to say that he was going to have to change if he wanted to move on to a more senior position.

At the first coaching session we discussed the reasons he found it difficult to socialise. In fact, when given the skills and the opportunity, he was rather good at it. At the weekend, the family visited his parents and it dawned on him why he lacked the ability to talk to people socially. His father did all the talking. No-one got a word in edgeways. And no-one in the family, least of all my client, had ever asserted themselves with their father or even tentatively suggested that others might want to put forward their point of view.

The last time I saw my client, it was as if a dam had burst. This insight about his background and the ability to cope with it had set him free. He was like a new man, chatty and positively effervescent.

There is often a conspiracy of silence surrounding bad habits in families. However, if you turn your back on your background without resolving what aggravated or upset you, it will come back to haunt you at important moments.

FAMILY GUIDELINES

I am a contributing journalist to *eve* magazine and a recent letter from a reader led me to produce the family guidelines below. This was the question.

Help! We should never have started it, but my husband and I have got into the habit of visiting one set of parents for Christmas one year, and the other set, the next. And – *quelle surprise* – now it's become impossible to break the pattern without offending whichever pair of parents is set to lose out. Not even either or both sets of parents coming to us is an option. Firstly, it's too long a journey for them all, and secondly, we're both in agreement that all we really want is Christmas with just the three of us. My husband works very hard and is often away, so my son (aged two) and I see him very little as it is. Yet the guilt of not making the trek up to Northumbria (his parents) or Somerset (mine) threatens to spoil our scaled-down plans anyway. What should we do?

My reply was around opening up discussions with all involved. In fact, let me reproduce it for you.

Christmas is a classic time for set routines. I know – I used to eat two Christmas dinners on the same day because of a similar impasse.

I am a great believer in involvement, which means asking both sets of parents to help with the dilemma. You could ask something along the lines of 'what can we do so that the three of us can be together as a family at Christmas but also keep you happy?' Then brainstorm the results. If they come up with a solution they are less likely to be offended by the result.

You can see from the start of this reply that I have been caught in similar family dilemmas. You do wonder how they evolve, but with a little prior planning, a lot of discussion with every-one and some vigilance you can avoid the worst of the fallout.

The allocation of domestic chores is another area that can often benefit from some family guidelines. So many working mothers still come home to families who expect their meals to be cooked and all domestic duties carried out for them. Stop now. Set up a code of conduct and cease to do any of the jobs you haven't agreed to do. Let the smelly socks accumulate, the piles of unwashed dishes grow to leaning towers of Pisa. Do not give in till you get some help from them. You are not equipping young people for life if they do not contribute to domestic duties. And that means both sexes.

Confidence comes from starting as you mean to continue and sticking to your guns even in the face of opposition.

SETTING THE SCENE

Now let us think about how you would like your family to look. I have put down some prompts, not so that you have to write anything in tablets of stone, but more as guidelines for the future. Things often just happen in life and before we know it we are moving down a path we have not consciously chosen but have fitted into like an old glove. Some advance thinking helps.

1. Behaviour towards one another

◆ How would you like to resolve disputes?
   ◆ By family discussion
   ◆ With both partners in agreement
   ◆ With the extended family involved

◆ How would you like to address each other?
   ◆ Asking, not telling
   ◆ Swearing, or not, in front of the children

◆ What should be the code of conduct?
   ◆ No violence, no physical punishment

◆ What times should you be together as a family?
   ◆ Meals – which ones?
   ◆ Family meetings – how often?
   ◆ Holidays – all or some together?
   ◆ Weekends – which pursuits could be family activities?

2. Domestic duties for the family. Some examples:

◆ Tidying bedrooms
◆ Cooking
◆ Clearing up after meals
◆ Washing dishes
◆ Washing and ironing clothes
◆ Washing the car

3. Personal duties. Some examples:

◆ Having a bath
◆ Washing in the morning
◆ Getting dressed
◆ Brushing teeth
◆ Rising on time
◆ Going to bed at the allotted time
◆ Arriving at school on time

4. Leisure time. How much time should be spent doing the following?

◆ Watching TV
◆ Being on the computer
◆ Playing or going out with friends
◆ Being with the family

5. Rewards. What rewards will they choose? Some examples:

◆ Pocket money
◆ Excursions to the cinema
◆ Extra time on the computer
◆ Time out on their bike
◆ Video watching

6. Which behaviours do you want to reward?

For example, choose from domestic and/or personal duties.

7. How much time do you want to spend with your own parents? Do you want:

◆ To spend every weekend or alternate weekends with one

or other of your parents? Or just Sunday lunch once a month?

◆ To spend Christmas at home with your spouse and children or with your parents? Which set of parents? Should they visit you or you go to them?

◆ How often should they visit you and for how long?

◆ What presents would you be comfortable with your children receiving from your parents?

Sometimes we need to stand back from our lives and ask ourselves if this is how we want it to look. So you do not have to have these principles as written guidelines, more as a guiding light. In fact, I remember a client of mine whose father was a psychiatrist and would post holiday rules on the wall of the children's bedroom with a timetable of events. It took her a long time to recover from this upbringing.

We should take just a little more time to look at how we handle our parents for a hassle-free existence, with or without children of our own around.

EMOTIONAL POWER WITH OUR PARENTS

Our parents are still influential in the way we behave as adults because of what we have learned from them in the past, regardless of whether we choose to see them frequently or decide to avoid them completely. If we handle them well and forge a relationship that is mutually rewarding then the emotional support gained will be well worth the effort. Of course there are always exceptions and where there has been an abusive relationship, limiting parental contact may be desirable. Apart from this, maintaining links with our paretns reminds us of who we are and the nature of our pedigree.

KEEP IN CONTACT

Even when we are adults in our own right, we are still children to our parents. They look out for us even when we are halfway around the world. I remember my father telling me that he got the atlas out to see whether the hurricane of the moment was going to hit the Cayman Islands where I was working. My parents were on a constant vigil over the television weather reports. If I had known, I would have telephoned more often to reassure them about my safety. So keep in touch on a regular basis.

ASK FOR SUPPORT AND HELP

They do live to help you. The trouble is that you may feel your independence means you cannot bother them. When times have been tough for me, I knew I could get unconditional love from my parents. And if you don't want the 'I told you so's', then ask them not to indulge themselves.

RESPECT DIFFERENCES

You may never share their taste in music, their political views or their moral stance, but you can respect the differences. In the past I have tried to change my parents' attitudes, and it always ended in tears. Now when pointed political comments are made, I try to let it wash over me or at least have a witty riposte.

ASSERT YOURSELF

One of the problems of always being thought of as a child is that parents still think they can tell us what to do. In the nicest possible way we must assert ourselves.

I remember when I was in my thirties taking my parents on holiday and going out with some friends one evening. I arrived back around midnight to find them awake and on the balcony of the apartment, just about to call the police. We went to bed having made arrangements for a conversation the next day when we had cooled down.

I pointed out that going out for dinner and returning at midnight was not an outrageous thing to do. I understood how they might have become anxious but they must in turn understand how I felt about being mollycoddled at my age. We then discussed some solutions and some of the potential consequences of not finding a solution when future holidays were being planned. In fact, instead of being irascible they were a little ashamed and apologetic. In the past I would either have played the martyr or become angry. Neither would have worked.

SO ASSERTING YOURSELF WITH YOUR PARENTS INVOLVES:

1. Setting the scene, recounting what has happened.
2. Understanding how your parents might feel.
3. Talking about how you feel.
4. Discussing solutions.
5. Looking at the consequences of a solution not being found as well as the harmony that would ensue with a solution in place.

SHARE YOUR GOOD FORTUNE

Your parents may be very well off and in no need of financial support but if that is not their position you could share your good fortune by taking them on at least one family holiday a year. Or have them to stay with you. This need not be an open-ended invitation. You can make it clear it is for a week or weekend. 'Time bounding' a visit is a must, with the length specified beforehand. Ignore at your peril.

The father of one of my friends would simply turn up on her doorstep and stay for indeterminate periods. While she loved her father, he had the less than endearing habit of grabbing the TV remote control and flicking through programmes while she was watching her favourites. He would also expect to be waited on, no doubt in the style to which his late wife had accustomed him. In short, he was driving her mad.

Normally, she would fume silently but she decided on a new tack after discussing it with me. She emphasised to him how much she loved him but also how his idiosyncrasies affected her and how she was finding it difficult to put her life on hold while he was there. She suggested she go on holiday with him for a week and that in the future she would want some prior knowledge of his arrival at her house.

In fact, when she shared her good fortune with him in the form of a week's holiday, he felt no need to turn up unannounced. He just wanted some attention and a little pampering.

DISCUSS YOUR FAMILY VALUES AND GUIDELINES

In order to sing from the same hymn sheet, talk to your parents about your family guidelines. These may not be their values but ask them to respect yours.

CONFIDENCE TRICKS FOR PARENTS

As a psychologist, I believe in doing what works. And what works is involving children by coaching them more than telling them what to do. They will not encounter a Victorian regime at school so you need to acquire the skills to prepare them for a life with more personal responsibility and freedom to put their ideas into practice. Here are some tricks of the parental trade.

BECOME A GOOD ROLE MODEL

To some extent, your children will be mini-versions of you. They will slavishly follow your behaviour and mimic it. Is yours good enough to be copied? If you swear, they will swear. If you are aggressive, they will be the same. A coaching style of parenting shows consideration and respect.

HELP YOUR CHILD TO BECOME A POWERFUL THINKER

You can create some circumstances in your family which will permit your child to become an independent and powerful thinker.

1 **Listen intently** to your children and respect what they say. It is so compelling to want to give them the wealth of your experience but the very essence of coaching is not to do that. Listen to their ideas no matter how outrageous or imperfectly formed they might be.

And do not interrupt. Given the level of stress around

today, it is so easy to want to hurry children so that we can move on to something else or, as it will come across to them, something more important.

2 **Ask, don't tell**. When you suggest this to some parents they often say they have no time for that. Of course, if a child has their fingers halfway down an electrical socket, then a bit of telling will work. But apart from these life-and-death situations, asking a child how they could have done something differently means they come up with their own solution. They are also more likely to remember what they did to get to the solution and learning is therefore swift. It just works!

I remember becoming irritated at my mother because she would ask me to find out how a word was spelt. This annoyed me as a child because I knew she knew it and it would have been so much quicker if she had just told me. But I had to go to the dictionary and laboriously look it up. Still, I grew to love words and literature as a result.

Ask searching questions. For example, 'if you knew you could cope with that bully, what would you do?' or 'if you knew you were just as intelligent as everyone else in your class, how would you study?' or 'if you knew you were as pretty as any other girl what would you do about going to the dance?' Then let them come up with their own solutions.

3 **Allow silence and solitude for thinking**. When children hesitate as they are thinking, it is so easy to butt in with solutions. Bite your tongue. Let them be. Thinking time is vital for your children so give them that space.

4 **Permit the expression of random thinking**. Ideas do not have to be perfectly formed to be expressed. In fact, thinking aloud is part of a creative process. At the Creative Problem Solving Institute in Buffalo, New York, blurting is a technique taught by experts. At conferences, they have to train us adults to blurt because we have been so well trained to keep quiet till we know we are right. All that achieves is conformity and a dulling down of creative ideas.

CREATE AN ATMOSPHERE OF APPRECIATION IN YOUR FAMILY

When we experience disapproval, we clam up. Look for opportunities to reward your children for even slight improvements in solving their problems.

I was speaking to a chief executive of a very successful company about how cool and calm he was in the face of chaos. I asked if he was like that at home. He said yes but that it wasn't seen as positive by his family. His wife and children viewed him as distant and inscrutable. When we tried to unpick what was causing this impression, he revealed that he would never reward his children with a compliment or attention unless they had reached their goal. He was astonished when I mentioned that the way to reward is by what psychologists call successive approximations, small steps towards the target. He really thought he was being motivational whereas his family perceived him as uncaring. He needed to reward more at work as well. When I was nearing the end of my project with the company, I heard that all the staff had been invited to attend an awards ceremony. I just hope he was doing the same at home.

Here are some rules for rewarding your kids:

RULES FOR REWARD

Intermittent
Specific
Immediate
Consistent
Genuine

Intermittent reward is what hooks the gambler, such is the power of this first rule. If you won every time you gambled, it would become boring and predictable. What keeps people glued to slot machines and any form of betting or gaming is that they never quite know when they might win next. So out of this addiction comes learning about the power of reward. In other words, catch your child doing something well, out of the ordinary or just better than usual, and field a compliment.

As has been mentioned before, for good learning to take place you must be specific about what you are rewarding. 'When you tidied your room today I thought it was great... finished your homework on time I was impressed...got up this morning without me yelling it was wonderful.' This is much better than saying 'You seem to be less irritating this week.' This statement is doubly unhelpful. It is negative and non-specific. How can your child learn from that?

Powerful rewards are immediate. As soon as you notice something good, compliment it. Don't wait till the evening, although you may want to praise again. Learning theory suggests that children need to pair the praise to their behaviour for the good stuff to happen again.

Consternation will ensue with cries of favouritism if you do not reward consistently. If one child has done something notable, make sure you are aware of the other's good behaviour.

People often mention that they hate praise or praising because no-one means it. They just want you to do something for them. Make sure that is not the case. Reward for reward's sake. It is an end in itself and must be genuine.

CRITICISE POSITIVELY

Not all criticism is bad. In fact, it is essential or children will start to exist in a cloud cuckoo land of approval, only to be hit by the real world. But it is important that it is delivered in such a way that the child feels you have given them the means to improve.

For example, saying 'You are totally useless at remembering instructions' is less than helpful. What do I need to do to change? It is not clear. I am left thinking I might be completely useless. It would be much better to say 'Yesterday you forgot to bring home the potatoes for supper. What could you do to remember next time?'

Some estimates put the recommended ratio of reward to criticism as high as eight to one. For every criticism of your child you must think of eight positives. I remember one father who realised that he had not said one positive thing about his teenage son for about eight years. Long hair, black leather and loud music had managed to obscure what was still his loveable son. As soon as he forgot about the outer layer, he started to show more loving behaviour to his son. And he responded. Both discovered music they had in common and started to attend concerts together.

CELEBRATE DIFFERENCES

Thinking is not a competitive sport. It is wonderfully collaborative. Morecambe and Wise, French and Saunders and countless other celebrity pairings build on each other's ideas. Differences are to be applauded, and diversity – be it race, colour, sex or whatever – adds spice to ideas. A competitive atmosphere creates tension, which is counterproductive to good thinking.

It is important to emphasise and reward the differences between siblings. When comparisons are made, there is always a winner and a loser. Much better to praise the strengths in each child.

COACH YOUR CHILD EMOTIONALLY

We now know that emotional intelligence matters just as much as general intelligence and it correlates highly with success. To be emotionally intelligent you must be able to know when you are experiencing an emotion and also notice when others are. It is also about motivation and forming relationships.

To find out how good an emotional coach you are, complete the questionnaire below. Be honest.

HOW IS YOUR EMOTIONAL COACHING?

1. Children really have very little to be sad about.

True / False / Don't Know

2. I think that anger is OK in the young as long as it's under control. **True / False / Don't Know**

3. Children acting sad are usually just trying to get you to feel sorry for them. **True / False / Don't Know**

4. If a child gets angry, they should be excluded.

True / False / Don't Know

5. When children are unhappy, they are real pests.

True / False / Don't Know

6. Stress is good for you. **True / False / Don't Know**

7. When children are unhappy, I am expected to fix the world and make it perfect.

True / False / Don't Know

8. I spend time helping children sort out their problems. **True / False / Don't Know**

9. I really have no time for sadness in life.

True / False / Don't Know

10. Anger is a dangerous state for children.

True / False / Don't Know

11. If you ignore a child's unhappiness it tends to go away and take care of itself.

True / False / Don't Know

12. Everyone has got to have some stress in their lives. **True / False / Don't Know**

13. Anger usually means aggression.

True / False / Don't Know

14. Feelings should be kept private in the family, not made public. **True / False / Don't Know**

15. When you notice signs of anxiety in a child you need to intervene quickly to help.

True / False / Don't Know

16. I don't mind dealing with a child's unhappiness as long as it doesn't last too long.

True / False / Don't Know

17. Helping my children cope with conflict is one of my parental roles. **True / False / Don't Know**

18. I prefer a happy child to one who is overly emotional. **True / False / Don't Know**

19. It is OK for children to show they are stressed.

True / False / Don't Know

20. When a child is unhappy, it's a time to problem solve. **True / False / Don't Know**

21. I help my children get over unhappiness quickly so they can move on to better things.

True / False / Don't Know

22. I don't see a child's unhappiness as an opportunity to learn much. **True / False / Don't Know**

23. I think when people are depressed they have over-emphasised the negative in life.

True / False / Don't Know

24. In my view, anger is natural, like clearing your throat! **True / False / Don't Know**

25. When a child is angry, they are very unpleasant.

True / False / Don't Know

26. I set limits on a child's anger.

True / False / Don't Know

27. When a child acts stressed, it's to get attention.

True / False / Don't Know

28. Anger is an emotion worth exploring.

True / False / Don't Know

29. I try to change the children's angry moods into cheerful ones. **True / False / Don't Know**

30. Getting angry is like letting off steam, releasing the pressure. **True / False / Don't Know**

31. When a child is unhappy, it's a chance to get closer. **True / False / Don't Know**

32. Children really have very little to get stressed about. **True / False / Don't Know**

33. When a child is unhappy, I try to help them explore what is causing it. **True / False / Don't Know**

34. Children get over anxious spells if you leave them alone. **True / False / Don't Know**

35. The important thing is to find out why a child is unhappy. **True / False / Don't Know**

36. When a child is depressed I'm worried they have a negative personality. **True / False / Don't Know**

37. If there's a lesson I've learned about unhappiness, it's that it's OK to express it.

True / False / Don't Know

38. I'm not sure anything can be done to change unhappiness. **True / False / Don't Know**

39. When a child is unhappy, I'm not quite sure what they want me to do. **True / False / Don't Know**

40. Stress is such an overused word; people just use it as an excuse. **True / False / Don't Know**

41. If there's a lesson I've learned about anger, it's that it's OK to express it. **True / False / Don't Know**

42. When a child is angry, I try to be understanding of their mood. **True / False / Don't Know**

43. When a child is angry, I'm not quite sure what they want me to do. **True / False / Don't Know**

44. When a child is angry, I want to know what they are thinking. **True / False / Don't Know**

45. When a child is stressed and anxious I just feel they aren't coping well. **True / False / Don't Know**

46. When a child is angry, I try to let them know I care no matter what. **True / False / Don't Know**

47. When a child is angry, I try to put myself in their shoes. **True / False / Don't Know**

48. It's important to help a child find out what caused the anger. **True / False / Don't Know**

SCORING

DISMISSING – Add up the number of times you said True for the following items:

1, 2, 7, 9, 11, 16, 18, 21, 22, 23, 29, 32

DISAPPROVING – Add up the Trues in:

3, 4, 5, 10, 13, 14, 25, 26, 27, 36, 40, 45

LAISSEZ-FAIRE – Add up the Trues in:

6, 12, 19, 24, 30, 34, 37, 38, 39, 41, 43, 46

EMOTIONAL COACHING – Add up the Trues in:

8, 15, 17, 20, 28, 31, 33, 35, 42, 44, 47, 48

If you responded 'don't know' more than four times, you may want to work at becoming more aware of emotion in yourself and others.

Now compare your four scores. The higher you scored in any one area, the more you tend to that style of parenting.

The ideal score for a parent would be zero in the **dismissing** and **disapproving** categories, with the highest score in the **emotional coaching** category and a few **laissez-faire** scores.

To **dismiss** or **disapprove** of a child's upset or anger is to make a child feel ashamed of the emotion and to foster the desire to hide it. You may feel that these emotions are amusing in one so small and adopt a teasing attitude. This is to denigrate emotions that are very strongly felt. Children are people too – just smaller.

High scores in the **laissez-faire** category mean you believe that expressing emotion is a good thing but not that you should intervene to do anything about it. This is fine but represents missed opportunities. Helping a child to talk about how they feel, understand the causes and work out where to direct the feeling, is what parenting is all about.

A high **emotional coaching** score? Congratulations. Of course, to be a good coach you have to be comfortable with a number of emotions. Sadness or anxiety may be more acceptable than anger, or vice versa. But remember, there are no good or bad emotions. They just are. So cultivate a non-judgmental approach to all emotions.

The Sickening Mind by Paul Martin talks about the pitfalls of not dealing with feelings appropriately. If you repress emotions such as anger, ulcers and cancer can ensue, but if you shout the odds, this correlates with coronary heart disease. So it is important for children to know what they feel and talk about it in a rational way. And if feelings are to be expressed, you must create an atmosphere of acceptance.

The real trick to emotional coaching is enabling your child to cope with issues and know how to calm themselves down rather than waiting for you to help them. Coaching fosters responsibility and independence.

Things to Avoid Doing as a Coach

◆ **Labelling a child** with put-downs such as 'don't be such a baby' or 'she's the quiet one' or 'he's the lazy brother' can stick in a child's mind for life.

◆ **Sarcasm** like 'so you'll be top of the class again then' when your child has obviously struggled is humiliating, increases stress and slows down learning.

◆ **Global criticism**, for example 'stop being a menace', is less helpful than saying 'you must not pull tins off the shelves in the supermarket'. Learning is achieved by helping children understand specific constructs.

◆ **Teasing and making fun** of a child is just as bad. It is saying their upset is trivial and laughable.

At a recent conference I was talking to the audience about motivation: what we had done to motivate and demotivate others. One participant told us that she had been confronted by a big brawny guy in a local restaurant. He introduced himself as one of her former pupils, who remembered her when she was his teacher. Apparently, one day she had picked up his briefcase and laughed at its state in front of the class. He particularly remembered that she had called it 'scabby'. He told her how humiliated he had felt as the family were experiencing financial difficulties and could not afford much. And it took him a long time to get over the incident. This woman was mortified. She had no idea.

So avoid excessive criticism of all sorts. It increases anxiety, undermines trust and destroys confidence.

Things to Do as a Coach

◆ **Be specific**, for example 'when you volunteered to help that was great'. If you reward specific behaviour, you are more likely to get a repeat performance.

◆ **Discuss their options not yours.** Even the most well meaning parent can inflict their problem-solving on a child. Signs of this are 'what you should do is...,' 'if I were you...'. It's much better to listen, then ask what options they think might work. Then respect their wishes.

◆ **Offer choices.** A friend has always allowed her children to choose the clothes they want to wear and the food they prefer to eat. It has sometimes led to interesting colour combinations and strange culinary juxtapositions, but who cares? They began to learn what worked for them and to form ideas of their likes and dislikes. So parental guidance is about offering choices, not impositions or control.

◆ **Be honest.** There is nothing worse than the discovery of a parent's 'do what I say, not what I do' philosophy. And avoid saying that you understand what your child is going through when you have not taken time to listen. Children are intuitive about such things so all credibility will be blown by lack of trust.

◆ **Be calm.** If you are embarking on emotional coaching, you do need to take time. You cannot be rushed or stressed. It might only be 10 minutes but put that time aside to be uninterrupted.

When not to Coach

If your child has committed a serious misdemeanour, you may have to go straight to disciplinary methods, not coaching.

Coaching can come later when you talk about how to avoid a recurrence of the bad behaviour.

If you are upset or tired it is worth choosing another time as you will not give your child the undivided attention they deserve. Also if you are stressed or have had a bad day, your coaching may be more authoritarian than you would like. If you are stressed most of the time, perhaps it would be a good idea to make some changes in your life.

SUGGESTIONS FOR HARD-PRESSED FATHERS

When I was interviewing chief executives for my last book, one of them recounted that his son had told him that the time they had spent together that week had amounted to eight minutes, and he was falling asleep for six of them. Fathers do have a problem if they are not around to see their children growing up. They become strangers in their own family and increasingly isolated. Work is so demanding and the fear of losing their job can keep them working long hours.

Here are some tricks for fathers with limited time.

Be Home for the Bedtime Story

Long commutes and huge workloads may keep you at work but you can try to be home for the bedtime story. It is a great opportunity to be creative and to share your favourites together. It is the quality of the interaction that counts, not just the quantity.

At a presentation skills course, I remember one father

being asked to talk to the group about a non-business issue. He chose to talk about selecting his child's first book. He felt this was so important that it would either switch his child on to a lifetime of delight in literature or act as a complete turn-off. Reading with a child can introduce them safely to a literary fantasy life and you can edit the dull bits and play up the excitement. It could relax you, too, at the end of a hard day.

Try to Have One Evening a Week at Home

It is so easy to get into the habit of working all the time and thinking that this is what is demanded of you. The trouble is that if you do not give yourself down time, thinking time or relaxation, then you work poorly. You think, a little like the alcoholic, that you are doing rather well. However, with no rest you are categorically not. I know this even though I haven't met you.

So take at least one evening off to be with your family. No work, no e-mails, no phone calls. Chill.

Cook Breakfast One Morning a Week

It may be your one chance to be domesticated in front of the children. For their development, it is important that they see that men, as well as women, input into the home.

Indulge in Weekend Family Activities

Some fathers spend their weekends ferrying children around like a taxi service but never get to join in with any enjoyable activities. Stake your claim to some family fun.

Coach Your Children From a Father's Point of View

There are two sexes with different viewpoints and attributes.

Without the involvement of a father or father figure children only get part of the story.

DEALING WITH A DIFFICULT CHILD

Confidence in your abilities can be tested to its limits by an unruly child. Make no mistake – it is a power struggle and one you must win. How you do it is key.

If you need to change a child's behaviour, put them on a reward programme. Even the most difficult child will respond in two to three weeks. Here are the steps.

◆ **Leverage.** Work out in advance what motivates your challenging child: a TV programme, going out on their bike, a trip to the cinema at the weekend. Make a list of whatever turns them on.

◆ **Desired behaviour.** Make a second list of how you would like them to behave: tidying the bedroom, brushing their teeth, washing the dishes; being pleasant to the others in class; helping others and not hitting them.

◆ **Construct a points system.** Now make a chart with the days of the week along the top and the desired behaviour down the side. Buy or make some gold stars for noting good behaviour and some black ones for the opposite. Work out a points system of rewards – one day's good behaviour equals a TV programme, two days equals a bike ride, a week earns a trip to the cinema.

◆ **Reward success.** When a child is behaving badly it is so easy to ignore the good times and get into the habit of constant criticism and punishment. This programme turns all of that around and focuses on the positive. Of course, if no progress has been made, there must be no rewards. Never capitulate or you will have lost the battle. You must be consistent, with both parents involved and singing from the same hymn sheet, so that one cannot be played off against the other. Believe me – your child will try every trick in the book.

One child I counselled was particularly challenging for his parents. He used to hit his head on the pavement outside the supermarket until he was supplied with sweets, and he also had the endearing habit of beating up small girls in his class just for fun. His first response to his reward programme was to steal all the black stars so that he could only get gold ones. It was a wonderful moment because we then knew he had bought into the system. Even he was as good as gold in three weeks.

The joy of all this is that you never have to lose your temper, which is so destructive for both you and your child. No progress, no rewards.

Parents give so much to their children, whether they deserve it or not. Always a bad idea. Let kids earn their pocket money. Get them to tidy their rooms, make breakfast, wash dishes. Then they will understand the value of money and its link with endeavour.

Children must make the link as early as possible between their behaviour and outcomes.

THE TEENAGE YEARS

This can be a time when hormones and parents rage in equal proportions. But it does not have to be this way. There are some confidence tricks here, too, that will allow you to live in harmony with the hormones.

◆ **Respect them as young adults.** Listening is more important at this stage than at any other time. Great tolerance of experimental dress and philosophies, and of excessive time in the bathroom is advised.

◆ **Let them have privacy.** If the bedroom is a mess, shut the door.

◆ **Encourage independent decision-making.** If you try to impose your will on a teenager, you are asking for trouble. All the families I know who foster independence can't get rid of their teenagers. They enjoy their freedom and have nothing to rebel against.

◆ **Surround them with a community.** Other friends, parents, ex-baby-sitters and relatives of all ages can act as advisers so that your teenager does not have to depend solely on you for support.

◆ **Let your children go.** Whether you like it or not, they will leave the family home one day. Long before that happens, make sure you have made a separate life for yourself so that your fulfilment is not entirely based on your children. If not, they feel that pressure and rail against it.

COPING WITH SEPARATION AND DIVORCE

I don't have to tell you that many marriages fail and the number of divorced and separated people has increased exponentially. It does leave children in a limbo of love, so what should you do?

WHEN MARRIAGE FAILS...

◆ Don't use children as weapons and don't ask them to take sides.

◆ Never name-call your ex partner.

◆ Be honest with your children and give them feedback about the progress of the divorce.

◆ Talk about the conflict and why it is happening. It is good emotional coaching.

◆ Provide additional support from other adults.

◆ Remain involved with your children's lives, even if you no longer live with them.

SINGLE PARENTS

Being a single parent brings with it distinctive challenges so I asked David, a friend and colleague, to provide advice for this section.

He became a single parent of an eight-year-old daughter and a four-year-old son when an 18-year marriage ended with his ex-wife 'moving in' with her friend Claire. There was no 'custody' battle – indeed it was never even discussed. He always jokes that this was the biggest (if not the only) compliment she ever paid him!

Over the years, many women (and a few men) have told him. 'I just don't understand how any woman could leave her children.' He says, 'I don't understand how any man could either.' His kids are regularly asked about this 'odd' situation by school friends and their parents, but they do not see anything unusual about it. To them, it's normal, and David thinks that 'normal' is a crucial word in parenting any children, as a single parent or as a couple.

He has a busy career and so he has to have some live-in help to get him through the week. At weekends, he takes over completely and enjoys doing everything with the children. Now that they are developing into the independent, self-managing, self-motivated, responsible, capable young people he has mentored them to become, he says that he must make sure he does not allow the 'empty nest syndrome' to get to him. He believes that with children it is definitely a case of 'you reap what you sow'. Here are his top 10 tips:

TOP TEN TIPS FOR BEING A GREAT SINGLE PARENT

1. Be open, honest and vulnerable when times are tough and you feel lonely.

2. Be kind, caring and considerate when your children are feeling bleak.

3. Be thoughtful and sensitive to their needs as they develop.

4. Be there.

5. Be there when they fall and celebrate the failures as well as the successes. They may go through a patch of failures.

6. Be firm but fun. Your children may be going through challenging times but beware of overindulgence.

7. Be a good listener as they may have to chat through loyalty issues.

8. Be interested and interesting.

9. Be a good role model.

10. Do not be tempted to remarry quickly just to give your children another parent.

TEN-SECOND CONFIDENCE TRICKS

◆ Show your parents that you care by telling them you love them once a month.

◆ In the face of sibling rivalry tell yourself 'I am unique'.

◆ If faced with your children's sibling rivalry, tell them they are unique and that you love them for that individuality.

◆ Tell your uncooperative child, 'I love you, but dislike your behaviour.'

◆ Remember you are their role model whether you like that thought or not. Before you shout, scream or swear, ask yourself if you want little versions of you running about.

◆ The last piece of confidence advice is to share all the above tricks with your children so that they can be as confident as you now are.

Now write your **confidence boosting action plan** as you review the chapter for the tricks that will help you.

4

CONFIDENCE AND FRIENDSHIP

Confidence and friendship are inextricably linked. Forming relationships is at the basis of every aspect of life – work, leisure, intimate relationships. The ability to meet new people and foster that contact into a friendship means that you need never feel lonely again. Even more than that, people buy people. This means that if you are either buying or selling something, you are much more likely to get what you want if you are likeable and perceived as friendly. This chapter will look at how to make friends and keep them, how to cope with arguments, how to deal with jealousies and how to work out when a friend is a friend no longer.

This chapter will also suggest that you entertain the idea of creating a larger group of friends. The advantages of this are:

◆ To enrich your life with those who have different pursuits and interests.

◆ To provide backup if one or two close friends leave to live elsewhere.

◆ To create a network so that friends meet friends.

◆ To have a mutual support group to give and receive help in a crisis.

◆ To avoid the lows in life by having a number of people to talk to.

Before we embark on that journey, answer the questions below to gain a better understanding of your current level of confidence in making new friends and how you interact with your current friends.

REALITY-CHECK YOUR FRIENDSHIPS

1. Do I make friends easily?...

2. When I meet someone for the first time, do I think about how to secure that friendship?...............

3. Is my circle of friends small or is it expansive?

....

4. Do all my friends come from my school days?....
If so, why?...

5. Do all my friends come from work?.......................
If so, why?...

6. Do I work hard at maintaining relationships by writing letters and e-mails, phoning, having people

⇨

round to my house?...

7. Have I lost contact with friends over the years?..
If so, why?...

8. Are my friends from both sexes? ....
If not, why not?...

9. Do I like all of my friends or are they in my circle
because they have always been around? ....

....

10. Can I rely on my friends to rally round in
a crisis?..
If not, why not?...

11. If I confided in my close friends, would it
remain in confidence? ....

12. Do I envy my friends?.......................................
How do I show that?...

13. Do my friends envy me?....................................
How do they show that? ....

14. Do I assert myself with my friends when they
do something that displeases me? ....

15. Do I feel genuinely liked by my friends?.............

RATE YOUR ANSWERS

Questions 1 to 5

This section is asking about the ease and breadth of your friendships.

If you answered no to question 1, this chapter is a must for acquiring the skills of forming relationships. Also, if you answered no to question 2 you might have found that, despite making many acquaintances, they never develop into friends because you need the skills to follow up that first meeting. Questions 3 to 5 are about how inclusive or exclusive you are in your friendships. Having an expansive network of old friends from school days, colleagues from work and new friends is the option that increases confidence.

Questions 6 to 9

If you have answered no to question 6, do not be surprised if you have a limited number of friends. You need to do the basics of keeping in touch and meeting up. If you have lost contact as in question 7, make a resolution to change that pattern. With question 8, if you have answered no to having friends of both sexes, ask why you have limited yourself. Part of achieving balance is having friendships that span all of your interactions with the outside world. If, in question 9, your friends have been around for a while rather than selected because you really like them, perhaps it is time for a revision. Having friends who have been in our lives forever is comforting but may also be limiting. It also means that we have not had to form friendships on purpose as they have always been there.

Questions 10 to 15

This section of questions reviews the quality of your friendships. If you cannot rely on your friends as is stated in question 10, perhaps you need to challenge that unreliability, look to the quality of the friendship you provide or form new friendships. If you have answered no to question 11 – about your friends keeping confidences – then a review is necessary. Answering yes to question 12 or 13 means you need to deal with the disruptive emotion of jealousy. Increasing your confidence and self-esteem will help you (see Chapter 1). If you have answered no to question 14, learn the techniques of assertiveness and influencing in this chapter. If you do not feel genuinely liked by your friends, as in the final question, ask them for feedback as to why that might be and perhaps embark on a process of personal change with the support of your friends or acquire new friends who reflect your level of self-esteem.

WHO ARE YOUR FRIENDS?

I am always amazed at the differing views there are about friendship. Some people will have no friends only family, others just one close friend throughout their lives, some a select circle, whilst others foster an open door, taking an 'all comers' philosophy towards friendship.

When I am coaching I often use a technique called 'The Train Exercise'. I ask that my clients draw a track and a train with carriages. On that train they then draw the most significant people in their life. Try it now on an A4 sheet of paper if you want to explore the technique yourself.

THE TRAIN EXERCISE

1. Draw some hills.
2. Draw a railway track.
3. Draw a train on the track.
4. Draw some carriages behind the train.
5. Draw the most significant people in your life on your train and name them.

RESULTS

Ask yourself the following questions:

◆ Who was on your train and who did you miss out?

◆ Were those on your train from your immediate family or did you include friends and work colleagues? If you missed out any group, why was that?

◆ Who did you draw first, nearest the engine?

◆ Who is driving your train?

◆ Is your train drawn with straight or rounded lines?

My hypothesis would be that the more people you have on your train, the more vibrant your social circle and the more relaxed you are socially. Also, if you are driving your train, you are in charge of your life and the direction it is taking. If your train is rounded at the corners and not created with straight sharp lines, you are more likely to be people-focused and friendly.

This is not rigorously and scientifically tested but is nevertheless a very revealing technique which can be used for discussion. I was recently given the opportunity to test these hypotheses when I was asked to predict who would win *Celebrity Big Brother* on British television. The participants were given the train exercise before entering the Big Brother house. I had decided that Melinda Messenger and Mark Owen were contenders to win. Melinda had an extended family on her train and was in the front driving it, but Mark had an even greater number of people on his train including the band, his grandmother and all his friends. However he was not driving it. Both of these trains, as distinct from those of the other participants, were rounded, not squared. Mark won that series of *Big Brother* as voted by the public, so the drawings were an interesting predictor of outcome.

Other Case Studies

One man had no friends at all on his tiny train, only his parents driving it while he sat in the back carriage. Even at the age of 30, he had evidently led a very sheltered life, ruled by his parents, who had never allowed him to bring friends home. All of this was revealed in his drawing. In reality he had a hunted look and appeared depressed. Even his clothes seemed to oppress him, as he was dressed in a slightly too small V-necked grey sweater. I came to the conclusion that he needed to be liberated from his current life and to acquire some friends.

One woman had no-one on her train except her family, and her daughter was driving her train. It does not take in-depth analysis to realise that her adolescent daughter was ruling her life to the detriment of her social relationships.

In both of these examples, as well as many others, these people had failed to make or maintain friendships for one reason or another. Family had taken up all of their time or smothered their ability to socialise. Most psychologists, certainly my professional clinical colleagues, would say that for a balanced life you need contacts in four sectors:

THE FOUR SECTORS OF LIFE

Personal

Family

Social

Work

This acts as a kind of insurance policy so that if anything happened to any one sector, you would always have support from another. The young man I mentioned before would have been devastated if anything had happened to his parents. That is understandable, but his grief would be compounded by the fact that he would have no resources to fall back on. We all need people, no matter how independent we are.

Some clients I have worked with will put a wide circle of friends on their trains but no-one from work. Of course, they may be unemployed, but many people who have been in gainful employment for years will not draw work colleagues on their trains. So are work friendships not significant for them? In reply, they would often make the distinction between true friends and the acquaintances they meet in the office. It is as if they have been forced together with people they would not choose to be with and have had to make the best of it. When this is explored, they admit to liking the majority of these people but still make the distinction between work friends and true friends.

This limited parameter of friendship in turn limits those who hold these views. For example, they may not want to go out to office parties, passing up the opportunity to meet those in charge and become more visible. As a result, they are not put forward for promotion. People at work feel the distancing that holding these views entails, and in turn might keep their distance. Why not call them all friends and socialise with those around you so the quality of your relationships is spread throughout your life?

Kimberley, a six-year-old child I know, called a meeting with her parents. She had done this two years before when they met in the kitchen for a feedback session about the way her egg had been boiled. She felt it had not been carried out to her liking. It had been either too hard or too soft and her requests for a three-minute egg had been ignored. She was four then. So it was with great anticipation that they approached this meeting. Kimberley wanted to discuss her forthcoming birthday party. She stated that she would like each invited guest to bring someone with them that she did not know as she felt she wanted to expand her circle of friends. Her bemused but delighted parents were only too happy to oblige.

What a good idea. We all get stuck in friendship ruts, so to expand your circle follow Kimberley's confidence trick for making new friends. Have a party, however small, and ask your friends to bring someone you have never met before.

THE PSYCHOLOGY OF FORMING FRIENDSHIPS

As human beings we are social creatures. What differentiates us from the animal kingdom is our ability to interact verbally. However, we have still retained our animal instinct or gut reaction and the ability to read non-verbal signals. So when we meet people we have an instinctive reaction of trust or distrust, of approach or avoidance. If we experience trust and think an approach might prove interesting we then tend to assess how that approach is being perceived by monitoring the other person's body language. All of this, of course, can take just seconds so we may be unaware of what is happening.

If all goes well and we are receiving interested signals in return, we will embark on a conversation. There are a number of essential ingredients here. We tend to look for shared interests or values we have in common. Disclosing information about ourselves and our experiences builds bridges and establishes a bond. If we are continuing to trade information and maintain interest, we may decide to continue this friendship.

There are a number of skills associated with meeting people and converting these encounters into lasting friendships. Here are some confidence tricks of the friendship trade.

CONFIDENCE TRICKS FOR MAKING NEW FRIENDS

1: Be Interested in Those Around You

As you go about your daily business, look up and notice the people you meet. We are all so focused on our own agendas that we forget who is at the other end of the proffered ticket or the cup of coffee. I am not suggesting you make every waiter a bosom buddy or a long-term friend, but if you get into the habit of talking to people it will become a habit, like breathing. Also, this trade of interest just makes daily interactions more pleasant.

I was talking to an airline stewardess recently and she was saying that some members of the public were constantly rude and denigrating. They demanded rather than asked and were aggressive immediately, even when proved wrong. It seems that the more we become stressed and rush around, the less time and consideration we have for other people. We must ask ourselves if that is right and if it is the way we want to run our lives. Confidence is about going anywhere and meeting every-one who takes your interest on the way.

2: Get People to Talk

The best way to get to know people is to get them talking about themselves. Asking questions kick-starts the process. And the type of question is important. In Chapter 2 we talked about using open-ended questions to get to know a prospective lover or partner. The technique is just as relevant here. Starting to talk to people is not rocket science. You do not have to be witty, clever or particularly impactful. Just interested enough to ask them something – almost anything will do. Some examples:

USEFUL QUESTIONS TO BREAK THE ICE

. . . .

What you are eating looks good. What is that?

How did you get an invitation to this event?

Who do you know at this party?

Dreadful weather, isn't it?

Where did you get that jacket? I really like it.

Where are you going on holiday?

And if these sound banal, who cares? Contact has been made. Men especially get confused about what works in the 'getting-to-know-you' stakes and put pressure on themselves to be the coolest and cleverest dude in town. The stress of this, coupled with an earnest expression more suitable to an excursion to the dentist, often puts paid to any success whatsoever. The simple rule here is **make the other person feel important** and you will successfully foster friendships.

3: Try Some 'Conversational Cement'

If you are rewarding in your conversation you are more likely to gain a friend. What this means is that you say something like 'Going to China must have been very exciting. My trip of a lifetime was going to South Africa.' You reward your potential friend's comment before moving on to one of your own. When this 'cement' is absent, conversation becomes stilted as remarks go into a feedback of silence which is usually interpreted as disapproval. And no-one wants to be friends with someone who disapproves of them.

A lack of conversational cement occurs when people compete for attention, wanting their comments to be given ascendance over the listener's. This runs counter to making friends. The goal of friendly interactions is for you to get to know the other person and to put them at their ease, not for you to impress.

EXAMPLES OF CONVERSATIONAL CEMENT

How interesting. My only example of that would be...

That must have been horrific for you. I have had nothing in my life to compare with that.

You must be very proud of your daughter. Mine is also the apple of my eye.

What a great story. The example I came across was...

4: Discover Shared Interests

When we are in the process of getting to know another person, we tend to seek out areas of common interest or shared values. Again, teasing out this information can be done with questions. Some examples are given below.

QUESTIONS TO DISCOVER SHARED INTERESTS

Who are you travelling with?

Who are you going to meet?

Tell me more about your family.

What do you do for a living?

Where are you based?

How happy are you with your job?

What would you really love to do?

What do you do in your spare time?

How did you become involved in that?

How much time does that take up?

Where did you go to school?

What did you go on to do after that?

How do you keep up to date now?

As you hear the answers, you can work out whether this person is interesting enough to develop a friendship with.

5: Try Some Self-disclosure

Forming relationships cannot be a one-way street. You must also give a little of yourself. Self-disclosure has a bonding effect. It builds bridges and lets your potential friend know a little of the content of your life. Revealing vulnerability also creates a closeness which can lead to self-disclosure from the other person in turn. It means that you trust this new-found friend with this information.

As a psychologist, my patients tell me about their personal

and family problems and I talk about similar situations I have gone through in my own life. When they have come through their particular crisis, they tell me that they felt I understood what they were going through. Self-disclosure helps to make that connection.

6: Notice Any Mirroring

When we are getting along with someone, we quite naturally and automatically tend to copy or mirror their body language. If, at the end of your conversation, you notice that you are both mirror images of each other's body language, then you have hit it off.

FOSTERING FRIENDSHIPS

Friendships do not happen just by themselves. Men, especially, tend to take their friends for granted. This may be due to men's orientation towards action and women's preference for dealing with people. The advent of e-mail, however, has changed this somewhat. That combination of 'information technology' and instant contact helps men to communicate on a more regular basis. But we must not forget that meeting up in person truly helps to foster friendships.

Here are some ideas to foster friendships and move people from acquaintances to close friends.

DEVELOPING YOUR FRIENDSHIP

◆ Talk about more than sport or fashion.
◆ Listen to a friend's story – not just the words but the meaning behind the words.
◆ Look for the good in your friend and mention what you value.
◆ Keep confidences.
◆ Share your good fortune if they hit bad times.
◆ Ask for help if you are in need.

I remember a client who came for help because she was depressed. It turned out that she had few friends and, as a result, no social life. When I asked about her friendships, she said she had given up on personal friends because she could not cope with their betrayal. They had let her down for one reason or another when she had trusted them implicitly. When we analysed the situations she had confronted, they were fairly everyday letdowns. We started to discuss why these might have occurred, and what transpired was that she was a very black-and-white thinker. A friend who could not make a dinner and cancelled at the last minute was never given a second chance of an invitation. Another friend who had breached a minor confidence was relegated to traitor.

We ended up realising that these mishaps are part of friendship. None of us is perfect. We make mistakes. All we need to do is find a way of coping. The next section looks at developing emotional power with friends so that friendships can be fostered, not flung aside.

EMOTIONAL POWER WITH FRIENDS

Below I have outlined eight scenarios and four or five possible responses. With as much honesty as possible, choose the one you would be most likely to do in real life. After each response I will discuss the most emotionally powerful alternatives because there may be more than one option.

1: NEGATIVITY ABOUT YOUR NEW JOB

You have just received the good news that you have been successful in obtaining a new job but a comment from a friend dismays you. He wonders how you managed to 'bullshit' your way with the interview panel and casts doubt on your ability to do the job. How would you respond? Would you:

   a. Become really angry but feel that it would be of little use to say anything. He is always saying things like this.

   b. Choose your moment and put him down in front of others.

   c. Feel quite justified in aggressively taking him to task.

   d. Secretly believe he is right and so say nothing.

   e. Ask why he made the comment because it has really irritated you.

Analysis

Let us assess the various responses to this scenario. If you chose a) you have all the disadvantages of feeling angry without communicating any of it. Keeping anger inside is not good for anyone. As I have mentioned before, emotional repression correlates with diseases like ulcers and cancer if it becomes a habitual response. Sometimes friends get into the habit of jokey put-downs which are fine while everyone is relaxed and happy, but when we are stressed we start to take these put downs seriously. Then no-one is laughing. Unless it is a one-off remark, you should really talk to your friend about how angry the comments made you feel.

If you chose b) you are embarking on a tit-for-tat policy which is considered passive-aggressive and 'games-playing' behaviour. The trouble is that these kinds of situations simply escalate, as your friend then seeks out situations to get back at you. This indirect communication does not solve the problem and, in fact, could make things worse.

If you chose c) you have decided on a directly aggressive response. You may feel justified, but there are risks in being so aggressive. It may jeopardise the friendship.

If you chose d) you are suffering from low self-esteem. You may feel lucky to have been offered the job but you can also feel you deserve it.

If you chose e) you are definitely more assertive than aggressive. Asking **why** opens up the dialogue, and talking about the irritation or anger you feel provides feedback about your friend's behaviour. It also allows him to apologise and/or change the way he communicates with his friends.

If he says 'it was only a joke', and you do not feel that is a satisfactory reply, as jokes in the wrong circumstances can be construed as put-downs, tell him that. Write what you want to say in advance and this will give you the confidence you need to get started on this conversation.

2: THE SAME JACKET

Your friend has turned up to dinner wearing exactly the same jacket as you. This has happened many times before. What do you do?

    a. Let it all wash over you. After all, it's only clothes.

    b. Say 'enough is enough' and ask vociferously what is going on.

    c. Mention in a quiet moment that it is a bit strange and it would be good if you did not copy each other.

    d. Make sure you buy something exactly the same as them on your next shopping trip.

    e. It is a compliment to be copied so you are more amused than irritated.

Analysis

It is safe to say, without being deemed politically incorrect, that this scenario is more of a problem for women than men. If both parties are happy to look like twins, there is no problem. But if one friend feels that they are being copied and their individuality is in question then something needs to be said. But how?

If you chose a) you are very relaxed – and probably a man, very likely one for whom clothes are not a priority.

If you chose b) you have opted to be aggressive, with all the associated risks for your friendship.

If you chose c) you are assertive and more likely to set up a dialogue about why this is happening. If your friend envies your taste, perhaps shopping together and helping to choose what suits each other would avoid these embarrassing twin moments.

A choice of d) means you are getting your own back without communicating your fears about looking like clones, and probably giving your friend license to do the same. You are not, of course, getting to the root cause of the problem.

Choosing e) shows great insight into why such copying occurs. It is usually carried out by people with low self-esteem who simply want what you have got. Increasing the friend's confidence might well work as a strategy. If so, move back to response c).

3: LATENESS

3. Your friend is always late for everything you do together. What do you say to them when it happens again?

a. Tell your friend that lateness drives you mad and next time you just will not be there.

b. Realise that it is just the way they are. They do this to everyone so it is not a personal slight. So you say nothing and take a good book to read while you wait.

c. Phone your friend's partner and tell them how their lateness affects you.

d. Find yourself protesting loudly about their timekeeping. After all, you had to have a few drinks to pass the time.

Anaylsis

Being late on a regular basis is not only indicative of disorganisation but it is also impolite. It is really saying that my time is more important than yours. Of course, everyone can be late occasionally – modern transport conspires to deliver that – but it's reasonable to get angry when it becomes habitual.

I have a friend who is infamously late. I was very relaxed

about it and had seen it as a consistent character flaw, with her lateness delivered to all friends in an equitable fashion. Until one day. She happened to be in a cab with me, going to meet the sister of a new boyfriend. For once I saw her keen to be on time. She was in such a flap, looking anxiously at her watch and rushing out of the cab so that she would not be late. Clearly she could be punctual, but we were not important enough for the effort.

So if you chose a) you have probably waited for this friend many times before and have decided to take the assertive path. It does not require you to raise your voice. Just state how you feel and what you will do in the future if they are late again. Then, of course, you must follow through and leave next time.

Choosing b) changes nothing and you will always be kept waiting.

A choice of c) means you are going behind your friend's back and giving the problem to someone else to solve. You are being indirect in your communication with that friend and this will not help to increase your confidence in this and similar circumstances.

Protesting loudly as in d) has all the risks of endangering your friendship. Only you can judge if it has got to that stage of irritation.

4: TAKE OVER

You are talking to an attractive member of the opposite sex and your friend elbows you out of the way and takes over. What do you do?

    a. Elbow your friend out of the way in return and carry on talking.

    b. Take them to one side and ask what they think they are doing.

    c. Wait till they are talking to someone you know they fancy and do the same to them.

    d. Think that your friend is more attractive than you and leave them to it.

Anaylsis

There are some friends who just want what we have. And you have to work out how to handle that if you believe the friendship is worth saving.

If you choose a) you have decided you have had enough and are resorting to aggression.

With b) you are being assertive and asking for an explanation of your friend's bad behaviour. This is the response of choice.

Option c) is the manipulative revenge response, which, like the previous ones, escalates the competition and resolves nothing.

Choosing d) means you have low self-esteem. This response should be outlawed as an option. Look at the following section, Dealing with a Jealous Friend, for some essential confidence tricks.

5: LENDING MONEY

You have lent your friend a sizeable sum of money which they have not repaid. You could do with it to go on holiday. Do you:

    a. Say nothing. They will realise in time that it must be repaid.

b. Ask for a loan for yourself from your friend that is the equivalent of your loan.

c. Confront them with the debt and demand its repayment with interest.

d. Ask why it has not been repaid and arrange a payment scheme if your friend is still in financial difficulties.

Anaylsis

Arguments about money put pressure on so many relationships and friendships. You can go through life with the adage 'neither borrower nor lender be' but reality is that at times we rely on friends to get us out of a pickle.

A choice of a) means that you are indulging in a bit of wishful thinking. Often we forget that we have borrowed money and a swift reminder is all that it takes. Never be fearful of reminding the borrower. Of course, if they deny all knowledge you must be prepared to give the details of when you lent it, for what and how much. These facts at your fingertips should generally win your case for you.

Choosing b) is the indirect approach, destined to make things worse.

Option c) is confrontational. It may get you your money back but it may also lose you a friend.

Option d) is the more assertive response and is the best choice if you have previously asked for the return of your money. If a friend has avoided repayment, it is probably for a good reason, so you need to find out why. And if financial difficulties persist, you can shout all you like but you will not be getting your money back. Much better to offer payment terms and then you can both return to the friendship.

6: UNSUITABLE MARRIAGE

Your friend is planning to marry someone completely unsuitable in your estimation. Do you:

    a. Say nothing and hope they will see the error of their ways.

    b. Try to show their partner up when you are all together so your friend will become aware of their shortcomings.

    c. Take your friend out for a drink and talk about your fears for the relationship.

    d. Speak to the partner and try to put them off.

Anaylsis

The choice of a) is very tempting. I have always felt uncomfortable commenting on a friend's partner. Everyone has different tastes and a frog to you could be a prince to your friend. So my first response is to say nothing and concentrate on their good points.

Choosing b) is pretty aggressive and fraught with difficulties. By 'showing up' the partner you run the risk of looking bad mannered and you may have two people hating you not just one. This is the route desperate parents sometimes take. As soon as you get into Mexican stand-offs, the parent will be the loser.

Option c) is a good course of action when you have noticed something that has to be divulged. For example, if the partner is married, going out with someone else or caught doing some nefarious deed, talking about it is an act of friendship. Even then, be very careful about how you approach these revelations. Relationship loyalty can be blinding to truth, and messengers have a tendency to get shot.

Choosing d) might well end your friendship faster than you

can say desperate. Because that is how it will be viewed – that and jealous. Whatever the perception, it will not get the desired result. In fact, it will probably bond your friend and your partner closer together.

Look at the section Friendships and Partners for more guidelines.

7: THE PASS

Your friend's partner makes a pass at you. What would you do?

   a. Make sure everyone hears your protests of innocence.
   b. Say nothing. They had been drinking and will probably not remember a thing about it in the morning.
   c. Speak to your friend about problems in their relationship.
   d. Have a talk directly with the partner.

Anaylsis

If you choose a) and let everyone know what happened, one of two things may occur. Your friend may feel you protest too much or that their partner is so unattractive that you are distancing yourself from the pass. Neither are good outcomes.

Option b) is a good choice if this is an isolated incident. Mistakes happen and friendship is easily confused with intimacy, especially if alcohol is involved.

Option c) could come into play if you have noticed a pattern of behaviour from the partner towards you or others. But remember about shooting the messenger…

Choosing d) would be a more targeted approach and you can open up discussions about feelings and boundaries without jeopardising the friendship.

8: BETRAYED CONFIDENCE

Your friend has been talking behind your back and betrayed some confidences. This has proved embarrassing. How do you handle this?

   a. Be determined never to talk to this friend again about personal matters.
   b. Talk to them about how this has affected you and the risks to your friendship.
   c. Start a damaging rumour about them.
   d. Feel justified in being very angry with them as they have betrayed you.
   e. End the friendship right now. They have gone one step too far.

Anaylsis

If you choose a) and never talk about personal matters again, why have the friendship? After all, that is what differentiates the friend from the mere acquaintance. Saying nothing to a friend is a little like not telling a restaurant about a bad meal and just never returning. You have denied them the opportunity to make amends.

The assertive response is b). If you talk to your friend about how this betrayal of a confidence has affected you, at least you have communicated your feelings and can make sure that if it does happen again they know the result. Also, it provides your friend with the opportunity to deny or admit to your allegations. You might just be wrong.

A choice of c) is passive aggressive. It is fighting fire with fire, which resolves nothing, turning your friendship into a combat zone. Why waste the energy?

The d) response of being justifiably angry may have right on its side but closes down dialogue, and you could end up being seen as the bad guy in all of this. That is always the risk when you choose anger and aggression over a more rational response.

If the betrayed confidence is not an isolated incident, the choice of e) – ending the friendship – is worthy of consideration. Take a look at the section When to Stop Being Friends.

AN OVERVIEW OF CONFIDENCE IN FRIENDSHIPS

Confidence comes from:

◆ Being able to deal with any eventuality. If you knew that you could cope with any situation, you would be so much bolder in your social life.

◆ Having a plan of action. We often try to resolve situations to no avail. Part of confidence is knowing you can move on to plan B, and if that does not work, what about plan C?

◆ Having an escalation strategy. If we go in to problem-solve with all guns blazing, where do we go from there? My view is that we should start pleasantly and escalate first towards assertiveness then aggression, but only if the pleasant approaches fail.

◆ Giving a friend the opportunity to change, as I am sure you would want to be given.

◆ Focusing on meeting this friend again without feeling guilty or ashamed of the way we have conducted ourselves, or worried that they might hate us.

DEALING WITH A JEALOUS FRIEND

Many of the above scenarios could be attributed to envy, and friends can be competitive. But if this gets out of hand, the jealousy that ensues can kill the friendship.

Fiona and Christine had been friends and neighbours for five years. Fiona, who was a few years older than Christine, had a party and invited all the neighbours, as well as Mike, a business colleague. Christine had stated earlier that she rather liked Mike and was looking forward to seeing him at the party. When most people had left, Fiona, Mike and Christine continued to chat. It became clear that Mike preferred Fiona to Christine, addressing all his comments to her.

The next day, Fiona bumped into Christine, who asked if Mike had a mother fixation, which might explain why he was more keen on Fiona than her. After gasping at the comment, Fiona managed to reply, 'No, he just likes me'.

The message of this story is that you do not have to let barbed comments hurt you. Nor do you have to ditch the friendship. Jealousy of some sort or another may enter any friendship. The error is in not handling it.

In general, you have two options with situations like these. You can either cope emotionally or problem-solve.

For the coping emotionally option try this 10-second confidence trick. Imagine that you are Teflon-coated so anything thrown at you simply slides off, leaving not a trace. We do not have to let undermining comments affect us. And you may feel that it is not worth asserting yourself as it may be an isolated incident due to thwarted expectation.

If, on the other hand, you feel that there is a pattern of jealous behaviour, the 'Teflon' option just becomes denial. There is an issue that you must at least try to resolve if the friendship is to survive. Try the following ingredients in your chat with your jealous friend.

Steps to Emotional Power with Jealous Friends

◆ **Be clear why you are upset.** When we are embarrassed we tend to skirt the topic and hint at what we want. Not all friends are perceptive and some may need more of a sledgehammer approach to problem-solving. To avoid denial and equivocation, tell them clearly what has happened, with dates, times and venues, and who was involved.

◆ **Talk about how this behaviour has made you feel.** Talking about your feelings is powerful communication. Your friend can't say to you 'don't be stupid, you did not feel that'. You know what the impact was on you, so share it.

◆ **Understand how they might feel.** It could be that there is nothing purposeful about how they have behaved towards you. If you suspect that to be true, state it. If, on the other hand, you feel that they want to bring you down to size, mention that you understand that your success of late has been a bit much for them to take.

◆ **How do you want the friendship to look?** Have some ideas in your mind about solutions to this issue. What would you like to happen? How would you like the friendship to proceed?

◆ **Discuss consequences.** If the friend continues to undermine you, copy you, be jealous of you, what might result? The obvious results are less closeness, less desire for contact, fewer confidences, poorer friendship.

◆ **Reward differences.** Be positive about your friend's attributes. Their behaviour towards you is fed by insecurity so make sure they know what you feel about their qualities and how they are different from yours. It is also good to end your discussions on a positive note.

DEALING WITH YOUR OWN JEALOUSY

The focus of this destructive emotion can be anything: weight, height, muscles, cars, houses, clothes, money, partners. It can be present at any age or even any stage of success. You just want what the other person has. However, what they have today could be yours tomorrow. Let that emotion galvanise you to greater things, or count your own blessings and be happy with your lot. We are all unique.

A helpful mind game is to visualise yourself with the same muscles, waistline, house or car and give yourself a realistic date for achievement. Tell yourself it is how you will be in the future, then work towards that date in a resolute way.

FRIENDSHIPS AND PARTNERS

Friendships can suffer if you do not approve of a friend's partner. You can make your feelings known, as was discussed in scenario six. And if your friend continues with the relationship, you must ask yourself if the friendship is worth sustaining.

Friends of mine, Bill and Steve, fell out over Bill's new partner James. Steve was used to going out with Bill every weekend and Bill had helped him financially when he had hit hard times. But when James came on the scene Steve felt usurped and did not want to share his friendship with someone he felt was not Bill's equal. And when Steve had a party he did not invite James to come with Bill. Bill was furious. And despite the close friendship they had for years, they now no longer talk to each other.

The arrival of partners often puts stress on a long-term friendship. Perhaps if Bill and Steve could have found a way to meet separately on some occasions and include James in some others, all might have been resolved. Of course, if Steve is jealous then that needs another discussion. Perhaps he needs to be more open about his feelings for Bill to discover whether they are reciprocated. Certainly both parties' lives are less fulfilled with the loss of their friendship. They both felt abandoned and have lost confidence in forming close friendships again.

CONFIDENCE TRICKS FOR HOLIDAYS

Friendships can become unstuck when you are in a friend's company day and night for a week or a fortnight at a time. What starts as a pleasant sharing of common interests often does not convert into a harmonious holiday.

I went away for a fortnight some years ago with two friends. It had been a last minute thing and I had not pursued the advice I am going to suggest to you. They both turned out to be closet smokers and puffed their way through their entire supply of duty-free cigarettes in the first week. I really dislike smoking. I had bought half a dozen bottles of wine to last the week but by the second day they had all disappeared, drunk by my friends.

One of them had also been on a mission to sleep with as many men as she could in the shortest time. So apparently our villa became know locally as the bordello. I can laugh about it now but I have not seen those friends for some time.

HOLIDAY TIPS

◆ Try a practice weekend before committing to a week or fortnight.

◆ Discuss likes and dislikes before going – restaurants, sunbathing, excursions and anything else you can think of.

◆ If you have rented a car, work out a driving plan so that one person is not relegated to driver and therefore no alcohol consumption.

◆ A bit of financial planning avoids conflict when you come to settle the bill.

◆ Know in advance what the sleeping arrangements are. If your friend is a snorer, take earplugs or some other device that limits the noise. Separate rooms avoid the issue.

◆ If you are both single, talk about what to do if either of you meets someone. Being thrown out of your room as your friend gets it together with the local talent can put a strain on the best of friendships.

WHEN TO STOP BEING FRIENDS

Sometimes you do have to let friends go. And that might be for any one of the reasons I have tried to capture below.

1 If your friend becomes an energy sapper you may feel that life is too short to cope. An energy sapper is someone who exhausts you with their negativity. They can be negative about you personally or about life in general.

2 If you find that a friend has been talking less than positively about you behind your back, the friendship can become strained. You may have taken them to task but it has made no difference.

3 If they were not there for you when you needed their help, you may feel that this negates your friendship.

4 If your friend has breached confidentiality in a major way, you may believe a friendship is untenable.

5 You may discover that you plain dislike them.

6 Life moves on and you may find that you have nothing in common or that you have ceased to share the same values.

However, friends do last a lifetime. I am finishing this chapter in Scotland at my mother's house. She is 80 and has recently been widowed. Her ability to bounce back from adversity is hugely helped by her ability to make and keep friends. They support and sustain her, and her social life is better than mine.

TEN-SECOND CONFIDENCE TRICKS

◆ When approaching strangers, a good trick for confidence is to say to yourself, 'I am worth knowing. I have had interesting experiences and have views and opinions worth sharing.'

◆ When you feel undermined by a friend, ask yourself if this is your problem or theirs. Use your emotional power to deal with the situation.

◆ Share a problem with friends. Take ten seconds to choose one friend you trust to give you honest feedback, and one who is creative. Phone both.

◆ If you feel jealous of a friend, use that emotion as a trigger for your own achievement.

◆ Share some ten-second confidence tricks with friends.

Now write your **confidence boosting action plan** as you review the chapter for the tricks that will help you.

5

CONFIDENCE
IN THE WORKPLACE

Work and home life have always blurred into one for me. I have had my own business for so long that the people who work with me have become friends, and friends have become part of the business. And so have clients. I do not mean coaching or counselling clients – these have to be confidential – but the directors of companies who hire me. When I changed my diary system to an electronic organiser, someone told me that I should categorise my contacts into business and personal. I couldn't make the distinction so gave up trying, allocating everyone to the 'all' file. And I have always worked at home in the evenings on projects or, as now, writing books. So it has been important to me to enjoy what I do and extract every ounce of fun that my business can afford me.

I do understand that not everyone is like me, nor would want to be. However, I do have a strong belief that work, whatever that is for you, should be fun. For a start, we spend so much time there. Even more important is the fact that we work so much better when we have fun. I am always amazed that companies remain oblivious to this astonishingly obvious fact. Forget gurus, leadership courses and business books. Make things fun, have a laugh and you get volunteers, not conscripts.

If you need evidence to be convinced, then Daniel Goleman, of *Emotional Intelligence* fame, talks in his book of an experiment in which a complex task was given to two groups of people. One group saw a documentary before embarking on the work, the other an episode of *Fawlty Towers.* Of course, the latter group performed significantly better than their counterparts in the 'boring' group.

Complete the questionnaire below to get a snapshot of your attitudes, feelings and current work skills.

REALITY-CHECK YOUR WORK

1. Do I really enjoy the work I do? ....
If not, why not? ....

2. Would I carry out this work regardless of the salary I was paid? ....

3. Am I proud of what I do? ....

4. Will I be happy doing this kind of work for the rest of my life? ....

5. Am I enthusiastic about my work on a Monday ⇨

morning or do I have to force myself to get up? .....
....

6. Did I make a decision to do this job or did I just
fall into it because it was available?.........................

7. Could I be better at what I do? ....
What would I have to do to be better?......................

8. Do I volunteer for challenging projects or do I
avoid them?...

9. Would I be happier in a different job? ....
If so, what?...

10. Do I respect my boss and the organisation for
which I work?...
If not, why not? ....

11. Do I keep up to date in my field by reading or
attending seminars?..

12. Do I present my ideas well at meetings?............

13. Could I be better at influencing? ....

14. If I were better at interviews, would I increase
my chances of promotion?...

> **15. If I won the Lottery today, what would I do tomorrow?** ....

Again, there are no right or wrong answers and only you to review the results. So be honest with yourself. Are you happy with your job right now or is there room for improvement?

RATING YOUR ANSWERS
Questions 1 to 5

This section is about your enjoyment of work, the job itself. When we are stimulated and feel that we are growing in stature in our chosen field, we are much more likely to be confident. If you have answered no to any of these questions then you may have to review your particular job or your chosen field. Many people have the view that a job is simply to earn money, but what a waste of talent and motivation for you to think this way. Of course you have to pay the rent or the mortgage and take care of any dependants you have but you can explore other possibilities. It is easy to underestimate your capabilities if you have been in a job for some time and have nothing against which to benchmark your skills. Five no answers in this section should motivate you to seek change as a priority.

Questions 6 to 10

This section looks at whether you are a volunteer or a conscript at work. If you have answered no to question 6 and have fallen into a job rather than making a conscious choice, you may have to reflect on whether this job will keep you interested over a period of time or whether you will lurch from job to job as you become bored. If you answered yes to question 7 and feel that you could be better at what you do, then do what it takes to become the expert. Question 8 taps into one of the core actions that correlates with success. Volunteering for projects, especially ones no-one else wants, and delivering the goods can earmark you for greater things. If you answered yes to question 9 and would be happy in a different job, start the process now. Lack of motivation can disappear when you are confronted with a new, more challenging environment. If you do not respect your boss and the organisation as asked in question 10, again, it may be time to move on or speak up to engineer changes.

Questions 11 to 15

These questions are more about the skills you bring to the workplace. If you answered no to question 11, you would not be unusual. However, to remain enthusiastic in your chosen field you need to keep up to date with latest developments or you will be bypassed by hungrier talent. Many people fear presenting at meetings, so if you answered no to question 12, read on for these confidence tricks. Similarly with questions 13 and 14, this chapter contains advice and skills to help you with influencing and interviews. Finally, if you won the Lottery would you continue to work where you are? If the answer is no, why remain there now?

I was reading Charles Handy's latest book, *The Elephant and the Flea*, and was struck by his comments in the third part of the book. His wife had asked him if he was proud of his work. He had replied that it was 'all right as work goes'. Her riposte was that she did not want to spend the rest of her life with someone who was prepared to settle for 'all right'.

We do sometimes settle for second or even third best. And sometimes we must leave a job so that we can be seen in a different light elsewhere. When you see someone around every day it is very difficult to imagine the potential of that person. A new environment allows you to reinvent yourself as the expert in your field.

You may have to negotiate to move jobs within your organisation, ask for promotion in order to be more stretched and challenged, leave for pastures new or start up your own business. All of these changes require some confidence tricks.

INSTANT WORK MAKEOVER

Write a two-minute list of your strengths. What are the particular cluster of skills you bring to your job or organisation? If you are cringing at the mere thought of doing this, then ask the friends and colleagues who make up your MI5 group to help you. Your MI5 group is your secret underground pool of helpers who will reality-test your ideas, provide you with honest feedback and support you in the political morass that comprises work. We are often unaware of what we bring distinctively to the workplace and may be pursuing the wrong jobs or selling the wrong skills. I will also bet that you underestimate your input.

Now write down your weaknesses. Do your strengths outweigh your weaknesses? They should – if not, add to the strengths list. When I interviewed 80 chief executives for my last book, *Fast Track to the Top*, they instantly knew their strengths and always had fewer weaknesses. What they told me was that you cannot be all things to all people and that there is not one-size-fits-all for becoming a leader. That self-knowledge allows you to understand who you can work best with and who can back you with the skills you lack.

I was speaking at a conference about different the personality types who were attracted to particular business sectors. Banking, I said, would attract a different breed of person to, for example, advertising. The organised, more detail-conscious person would suit the former and the more off-the-wall and creative type would be drawn to the latter. The point I was trying to make was that when you communicate, you must think like a listener.

No sooner had I finished when a female investment banker rushed over saying that she had scored very highly on creativity and low on organisation on a personality test. What she had to do in the bank's obsessional culture was to make sure that she surrounded herself with people who could do the bits of her job she detested and was not very good at.

So exult and capitalise on your strengths, and either work on your weaknesses by acquiring the right skills, or get someone with the skills you lack into the team.

THE VOLUNTEER EXERCISE

You may want to beaver away unnoticed for years doing the same job but, since you have bought this book, I suspect that you would rather progress and make an impact. Interviewing business leaders, I learned that what had made them successful was volunteering for a project and delivering results. You can do the same.

CHECKLIST FOR BECOMING A VOLUNTEER

◆ Look out for a part of your job where you could make a real difference. Perhaps historically the company has had poor leadership, poor performance or simply has not flourished, or you may have noticed a gap in the market.

◆ Put forward your ideas.

◆ Volunteer at least a percentage of your time.

◆ Deliver to deadlines.

◆ Be prepared to present your results.

INTERVIEWS

If you wish to be promoted, you must first become confident at interviews. And one of the major things to remember is how poor companies are at the interviewing process. Interviewers often talk so much you wonder how they can ever get to know the candidates at all. In fact, they probably don't. Poor companies usually adopt a policy of choosing 'people like us', like-minded individuals who will fit straight in. If you can get information in advance about the company you are visiting, give such organisations a wide berth. Ask current or previous employees for the inside story.

And do not ever take the view that any old job will be good enough. Or that a job in the hand is worth two in your dreams.

The *Sunday Times* list of the best companies to work for is a good starting point for your research. You may think you want any old job but once you are there your expectations rise, and if the job does not foster and stimulate you then you will turn into a coffee room moaner. You may also fall into the **take it now** trap. 'I will just take it now and leave when I get a better offer.' Ten years later you are talking about that retirement watch because that is all there is to look forward to!

PSYCHOMETRIC TESTS

Many people tell me how worried they are about psychometric tests. These are personality profiles or skills tests that help an interviewer to get to know you and look for skills relevant to the job.

There are some guidelines you can follow so that you feel confident and in charge of the process.

Five Psychometric Principles

1 Do not try to be anything you are not. The tests are set up to detect if you are either lying or putting yourself forward in an unrealistic fashion. Also, why would you want a job that did not suit your personality or skills?

2 Always ask for a copy of the results. It is your right to be able to comment on the written report. It is, after all, statistical, usually computer-generated and therefore fallible.

3 You could also ask what the weighting of the report is on the interview process. In other words, how important is the test in determining their choice of candidate? A good company should reply that it helps them to ask the right questions at interview. If more importance is placed on it than that,

then they are not using psychometrics properly. They should be used as guides, not tablets of stone.

4 If you can remember the test name, you can report the company to the test supplier, who should intervene and offer more training if the test has not been administered properly.

5 Do as many practice tests as you can so that they do not faze you when you are given one. They are really good fun and extraordinarily helpful to get to know candidates quickly. I can't imagine why companies do not use them more often. And a good company will use them wisely.

PREPARING FOR AN INTERVIEW

Let us now look at what will increase your confidence at interviews, starting with the preparation.

Research

Call them old-fashioned, but companies like you to be interested in having a job with them, not just any job that has been advertised and taken your fancy. This requires you to carry out some research into at least what the company does. Even better to know about:

◆ the market share in their sector
◆ where they operate
◆ who is in charge

Websites nowadays have oodles of information, as do the business pages of newspapers. So get reading and mention your research casually during the interview.

As an interviewer over the years for my own business, I've found that there is nothing more compelling than someone who has gone to the trouble of getting to know what you do and where you have done it. It is flattering and will get you everywhere. Well, at least an invitation to the interview.

It is also worth researching yourself. I know of many successful executives who have reached the dizzy heights of the boardroom by constantly being promoted internally and negotiating great financial packages for themselves. They told me that before an internal interview they go to a number of head-hunters to find out their worth in the marketplace. They may never use the information directly but it gives them a sense of self-esteem and worth. Some said that they repeat this process annually for an ego boost. Knowing your worth stops you feeling stuck.

Prepare for Questions in Advance

You know the kinds of questions they will ask you. It is no use looking like a startled rabbit in the headlights of a car when they ask you why they should hire you for the job rather than someone else. You must have an answer ready with some fluency attached. Prepare some answers in advance. There are tricks you can use to make this process easier.

1 **Learn how to use Mind Maps**. If you don't know about mind maps you should. Buy Tony Buzan's *The Mind Map Book* and follow the instructions. For those of you who know about Mind Mapping and have been on the courses but can't be bothered using it, start right now.

The advantages are many and varied. Mind Mapping is speedy and allows you to put all your questions and answers on one page. It permits flexibility, which linear note taking does not. And because it taps into the way our minds work, you remember the information much more readily.

So for our purposes here, put 'you' in the centre and radiate lines starting at one o'clock, writing the questions along each line in capitals. Now you are ready for the next trick.

2 **Prepare four replies for each question**. For example, if you were asked 'How would your boss describe you?', you might want to say hard-working, creative, good at problem-solving and calm in a crisis – whatever your strengths are. But give at least four – all positive, of course. We will come to weaknesses later.

3 **Provide examples or case studies.** It is no use saying that you are good at problem-solving and then giving no examples of your prowess. Why should I believe you? I may want to, but give me the evidence. So have some pet case studies that you can quote succinctly. Do not drone on. Practise being crisp. These stories should be about mastery, so focus on achievements.

I was asked to work with a former MP for a television programme about what became of ex-MPs. He had just lost his seat and was searching for a job. None had been offered. I quickly understood why when I saw his CV and subsequently interviewed him.

He had listed all the committees he had chaired as if that alone would impress. There was absolutely nothing about what these committees had achieved, and I presumed that they had achieved something. So activity alone is not sufficient – you must focus on outcomes and successes.

4 Use this list of typical questions to plan your answers

Opening Gambits

◆ **Chat me through your CV.**

◆ **What are the highlights of your career to date?**

Remember, these are selected highlights. You can leave out the in-between humdrum bits. The interviewers want to hear what you deem to be important, so be succinct. I remember with exhaustion one interviewee who never got past these opening questions as she talked without drawing breath for half an hour. She came across as more than slightly deranged. So avoid verbal diarrhoea at all costs. Concentrate on the following:

◆ any increase in turnover or profitability for the company
◆ how you have managed individuals or a team
◆ quality improvements
◆ deadlines reached
◆ staff developed
◆ crises avoided
◆ projects completed

Experience

◆ **What have you achieved so far?**

◆ **What goals would you like to have reached?**

◆ **Why do you want to leave the company you are with now?**

It goes without saying that you must focus on positives, especially when asked the last question. If you start condemning your last employer, the interviewer will be less than impressed. Concentrate instead on progressing to the next stage of your career, more responsibility, fresh challenges...

Learning – Past and Present

◆ How do your qualifications relate to this job?

◆ What do you do to keep up to date in your field?

◆ What courses have you attended recently?

Employers want to know how you have applied your learning so that they can take advantage of your skills. They also want to know that you are a work in progress, that you have further potential they can tap.

People Skills

◆ Give me an example of someone you have influenced recently.

◆ Tell me about how you have persuaded someone to do something they were unwilling to do.

◆ How do you motivate your team?

◆ How do you think you are influencing me?

Be prepared to give examples of past successes with people. If situations elude you, ask colleagues and friends. It always amazes me how everyone else remembers our successes, especially mothers, while we are more likely to dwell on our failures.

That last question may be a little tricky. If asked it, you have a good interviewer on your hands. Don't panic. Just notice their body language – has it been positive or negative? Have they smiled at you or withdrawn eye contact – that sort of thing. They are trying to assess how perceptive you are.

Ability to Work Under Pressure

◆ How are you aware when you are under pressure?

◆ What do you do to reduce that pressure?

◆ How do you recover after a setback?

◆ What signs and symptoms of pressure have you
   noticed in others in the past?
◆ How healthy are you?

The interviewer here is trying to discover how you look after
yourself and also how positive and resilient you are when
deadlines have to be met or setbacks occur.

Hobbies and Leisure Activities

◆ What hobbies do you have?
◆ What was the last book you read or film you saw?
◆ How do you spend your weekends?
◆ What sport do you play?
◆ What interest do you have in the arts?

All work and no play makes you a dull person. Organisations
are looking for well-rounded individuals who will be able to
relate to a wide variety of people, especially if they are going
to interact with clients and customers. An interviewer does not
want to hear that you work, sleep and get drunk on a Friday.
This may seem a trifle unfair if they load you with so much
work that all you have time to do is work, sleep and get drunk
on a Friday. But that's the way it is.

Weaknesses and Limitations

◆ What are your weaknesses?
◆ Tell me about a time when you failed with a project?
◆ What have been the most challenging situations you
   have coped with?

Be honest: everyone has weaknesses. However, an interviewer will want to know what you have done to confront
limitations and improve your performance.

As for the last question have a good story to tell. One, if possible, that has a happy ending.

5 **Know your unique selling point.** Understand what is special about you. What is this company getting for its money when it acquires you? An interviewer wants to know if you have an awareness of your special strengths. Go back to the exercise at the beginning of this chapter and choose your favourite strength from your list, checking with your MI5 group that this is the correct one.

DURING THE INTERVIEW

The major trick to use during interviews is to be as relaxed as possible. Obviously you are not going to be so laid back that you look as if you don't care, but you can be relaxed and dynamic.

When you are relaxed everything comes together. Your body language matches what you are saying and you are able to focus on the interviewer, not your inner anxiety. To achieve this inner calm requires a little work.

The old 'eggs in one basket' rule applies here. Make loads of job applications so that the one you really want is not an isolated case that you can get in a panic about. I know from my own experience that I always did a wonderful interview for the job I did not want. The company would pursue me relentlessly, determined to hire me. Whereas the one I wanted got a quivering wreck they could more than happily ignore.

A great **mind game** that really works is to visualise that you have already been offered the job. You imagine yourself behind the desk in your new office. Tell yourself that the job is yours and all you have to do is get through the small hurdle of an interview.

Then you visualise the interview. Imagine arriving and feeling confident, then entering the room, calmly looking round and appraising the interviewer/panel. Visualise the first question and your answer. It is received well. Then imagine the same response to all other questions. You are enjoying the process. You have planned some of your replies and you take time to think about the others, but you answer honestly and positively. You really get the feeling that they like you. The interview is ending and you feel that it is the best you have ever done. You are sure they are going to offer you the job. You see them shaking your hand and stating how impressed they have been with your interview.

At each stage you visualise mastery. Remember, this is not far-fetched. An interviewer wants to find a solution and you are it. As soon as you imagine success, it paves the way for it to happen. You simply have been there before.

So why does this work? Our brains are 'programmed' not only by what we see and hear but also by our imagination. Many studies have shown that the brain cannot tell the difference between input from the real world and input internally. So visualising success creates a path for success.

A **body language trick** for interviews is to look enthusiastic. You know to wear your favourite suit, shake hands, smile and all that stuff. But one of the important things to get across is your delight in the job and the company. People often make the mistake of thinking that they must look as relaxed as possible, which makes them sit back in the chair in a kind of sprawl. It may feel comfortable inside you, but it comes across as couldn't-care-less to the interviewer – not the impression you are striving for.

So what you must do is lean forward slightly, elbows on the table, gesturing while talking, and smiling and tilting your head to the side while listening. Now, if you are enthusiastic you tend to do this naturally, but since when did you feel natural at an interview? You need to do these things on purpose in this particular situation. Sprawl when you get back home.

AFTER THE INTERVIEW

If you get the job, who cares about 'after the interview'! But if you don't, you still have a little work to do. You need to find out why.

Ask the company the following questions. If they do not want to answer them, they will tell you. But this feedback is like gold dust and will lead to your eventual success.

After the Interview Questions

◆ **Why did I not get the job?**

Prompt with:

◆ **Were my qualifications not appropriate?**

◆ **Did my personality not fit the team?**

◆ **Was I lacking the requisite experience?**

Then:

◆ **What would I have to do now to get this or an equivalent job in the future?**

A good company will take time to give you feedback; a bad one will ignore you. Never assume anything about an interview. So many people I have coached have landed an even better job after they were told to get a little more experience in their area of expertise. Feedback reality-tests the impression you created, and it's far better knowing the truth than imagining the worst.

NETWORKING

Many jobs come about through a network of friends and acquaintances. Most people would rather give a job to someone they know than to a complete stranger. It cuts down the risk of it going horribly wrong. The devil you know and all that.

If you are going to job hunt through the people you know, do think about the impression you create. It is good to accentuate your unique qualities but make sure you are not so off-the-wall that people worry about you fitting into a team or company. The following story is a cautionary tale.

I was at a book signing of my first confidence book, *Confidence in Just Seven Days*, in Oxford Street. A German student in the audience had asked some interesting questions about research into confidence and self-esteem. After my short presentation, she came to talk to me. She wanted a job working in my company. As she was speaking, I became aware of some movement around her chest. She was wearing a low cut tee-shirt and, of course, I didn't want to stare so I ignored it. But there was more movement till I noticed a small set of whiskers appearing over the edge. I had to say something. Had it got in there by mistake? Did she know about it? How could she not! When I pointed out tentatively that she was harbouring a rodent in her cleavage, she was only too delighted to tell me about Snowy, her pet rat, who used this unusual mode of transport when they went out together. One could only hope it was chest trained.

When next day she phoned my office to ask if I remembered her and to reiterate her desire to work as a psychologist with the company, I felt that I should be fair. I asked round the office if anyone thought that we should employ a student who kept a rat in her chest. On balance, they thought not.

So she was right to ask about opportunities. Of course I remembered her, but make sure the memory enhances your job prospects.

MEETINGS, MEETINGS, MEETINGS!

Interviews are a necessary evil in order to progress to a more senior post or move to another company, but meetings are where you will be judged, either as a contributor or as a chairperson.

We spend so much time at work in meetings. Someone once calculated just how much that came to in monetary terms. The total escapes me but it was a huge amount. So there needs to be a good reason to have a meeting, the right people should be there, and it should have time limits and a certain liveliness which stimulates those attending to go and do things as a result. Does this sound like rocket science to you? Yet how many people rush to meetings eager to participate, keen not to lose a minute of the process? Sadly, very few.

In this section we are going to explore meetings from two points of view: that of participant and that of a chairperson.

MEETING TRICKS FOR PARTICPANTS

◆ **Make sure you have the agenda in advance.** You will then be able to prepare a response to important items or ones that concern you.

◆ **Arrive early.** The chairperson may be the only one there, so you can chat and get your opinions across directly.

◆ **Contribute.** Involvement is key to your success. Do not leave your views till afterwards, when the air will hum with insurrection. Speak up in the meeting.

◆ **Present well.** If you have to make a presentation, make it interesting. If you are an accountant, that could be your greatest challenge. One major trick is never to present a spreadsheet as an overhead. Select highlights for slides and hand the group the spreadsheet. They can see it better on paper, believe me.

◆ **No lap tops.** Do not respond to your e-mails, write to your mother or even finish a report in a meeting. It is rude. Even if others are indulging, do not do the same. People imagine that they can do two things at once, but in reality they do both badly. I have known meetings where each person round the table was concentrating on their keyboard as someone droned on in the background. Why have a meeting at all? Just e-mail each other.

◆ **Ask for a summary if none is forthcoming.** A summary of what has happened during the meeting as well as a round-up of actions and responsibilities, is essential for a meeting to fulfil its purpose. If the chairperson has forgotten, a reminder is worthwhile.

Emotion abounds in the workplace but everyone behaves as if it were outlawed. And the natural habitat for emotion is at a meeting. Most workplace bad behaviour can be found around a table of peers.

MEETINGS TRICKS FOR CHAIRPEOPLE

When you are successful at interviews, you will be promoted and have to run your own meetings. You could certainly make a difference by running interesting, zappy, short meetings.

Meetings Makeovers

◆ **Halve the meeting time. It creates urgency.**
◆ **Supply bacon rolls for those who arrive on time. The smell alone will drive people mad.**
◆ **Do something different, like getting participants to draw a picture showing how their week has gone. Give prizes for the best attempts.**
◆ **Brainstorm ideas in the meeting.**
◆ **Let people try out their ideas and take responsibility for them.**

Despite your best intentions, you may come across the occasional team member who is difficult. Confidence in the workplace is about having some strategies in place to deal with adversity if and when it arises.

Below are some different characters you may experience in meetings and some suggestions as to how best to handle them.

The Devil's Advocate

They start most of their sentences with 'let me be the devil's advocate here...'. They like to give a worst case scenario for just about everything. It is all a bit of an intellectual exercise.

The Trick

Devil's Advocates can be quite useful as they offer a contrary opinion. So celebrate that difference but bring in others of differing views so that they cannot hog the stage.

If they reiterate their views, point out that everyone has heard them before and it is time to move on with the agenda. They will need some quite tight control measures. Do not shrink from interrupting even when they are in full flow.

The Meganeg

They always see the worst of any situation and feel they have to tell people. They are great harbingers of doom. If you know the Rev I.M. Jolly, played most Christmases by Rikki Fulton or a representation of Scrooge, that's him! They look and sound depressed – and everyone else does too once they have finished.

The Trick

You must give them a chance to air their views but if you allow them to dominate the meeting, those attending will wish they hadn't. These people are the opposite of motivating. They are black holes of energy.

It is worth having a conversation after the meeting to find out why they appear so depressed. Some coaching or, dare I say it, counselling, might be worth pursuing. Certainly, feed back to them how they come across to you and the group. If work is the source of their depression, discover what kind of project they might find more positive and stimulating.

The Cynic

'Yeah, yeah, we tried that in my last company.' They have seen it all before. Nothing is going to get them excited. People wilt when they start their world-weary litany...

The Trick

Cynics think they are sophisticated and as a result better than other people. Of course, we are not fooled by that one. We know that really means they are insecure. Cynics have often been passed over for promotion and are probably way past their sell-by date. The only power that they have is that they have been around longer than other people and can scupper any new idea with their air of knowledgeable negativity. And, oh boy, do they use that power.

They need quite a lot of work, mostly outside the meeting room. You can find out what motivates the cynic, or at least has motivated them in the past. Involving them in projects, rewarding them and making them more acceptable to the group all helps. A word of caution, however – they may need to be encouraged to try pastures new as there comes a time when such employees are simply burnt out in their role. They are bored and lack stimulation. That conversation may be challenging but a bit of honesty about their contribution could be helpful. Of course, you cannot just get rid of them without good cause and proper procedure, but you can have a friendly chat about their behaviour.

The Rambler

'Was it Monday? No, I tell a lie it was Tuesday because I remember when I was in my car...or was it Wednesday?' Ramblers are pathologically unable to keep to the point and go into loads of inconsequential detail. Others are often numbed into submission and glaze over but it doesn't stop a rambler.

The Trick

Give a rambler a strict timescale to adhere to. If they overrun, then the meeting proceeds to plan. It will take only a few meetings for them to realise they will have to be succinct.

This does not have to be carried out aggressively. You can have a word beforehand to tell them what you plan to do. And give them feedback about their performance at meetings. Some presentation skills training may also help.

Reward them for even small improvements.

The Axe Grinder

No matter what the topic they always bring it back to the same axe they have to grind, the issue that they feel people have never quite taken into account. They bring it into any and every conversation, and certainly every meeting.

The Trick

The problem is no-one ever listens to the axe grinder and no-one has been listening for years.

You could make a difference by taking some time to listen. If something can be done, put the axe grinder in charge of the solution. Then, when they bring up the topic again, and they will, as old habits die hard, you can ask them to talk about the solution they are working on at the moment.

The Emotional Person

They are overwhelmed by their emotions – they may be upset, angry, worried, hurt all in the one meeting. And they can remain in emotional mode for long periods of time. Just being rational seems not to be an option for them and they tend to lurch from crisis to crisis.

The Trick

It is worth taking time to find out why this person is so emotional. Are they always like this or is their upset behaviour in response to things going on in their life or at work?

Some training or coaching in stress management and influencing skills could help them to talk about issues without becoming so off-puttingly emotional.

I remember one young woman I coached who became so anxious about meetings and one-to-one interviews with her boss that she would burst into tears when she heard even a whiff of criticism about her work. Her behaviour could be traced back to her parents being very punitive and perfectionist.

The way I suggested she overcame her emotionality was for her to take breaks in the meeting so that she could relax. At the same time she learned how to think more positively about her contribution. Gradually, the tears stopped and she gained control of her emotions.

The Enthusiast

They get carried away with every new idea anyone has but especially their own. They will bounce their way through a meeting unable to understand why people might have any reservations and utterly sure they will come around in the end.

The Trick

You don't want to dampen anyone's enthusiasm but you may have to curtail some excesses.

Dealing with the group's reservations and brainstorming ways round them till you come up with an agreed action plan is good meeting practice. Put the enthusiast in charge of this process. They will be so busy facilitating the group that they won't have time to pursue their own goals.

Training them in good meeting practice will reveal to them that you cannot just be positive, you must also be practical.

The Steamroller

These people have power and status. They believe they have the best ideas and that if they speak loudly enough, people will just do as they are told. They don't find listening necessary as they have authority and will do what they want in the long run.

The Trick

Steamrollers are often to be found at the top of organisations so it could be that the steamroller is the chairperson of the meeting. However, they may be part of your meeting as many companies have a matrix structure in which people are called together for projects. So someone more junior may be leading a meeting because they, rather than their boss, have the expertise.

One of the ways to limit the steamroller's behaviour is to go back to the group for approval of any action. Running with the consensus helps to shift the power away from them.

If that doesn't work, you could outline the way the meeting works in terms of everyone making a contribution. And if that fails to get results you may have to have a chat after the meeting and provide feedback about steamroller behaviour. Given that this person may be senior to you, always remember to be assertive rather than aggressive – if you want to keep your job that is.

Other Tricks

The trick with meetings is:

◆ to control the debate pleasantly, making sure everyone has their say but not being afraid to assert yourself to keep to the agenda, even with people more senior than you.

◆ to do a lot of one-to-one work before and after. Giving feedback about meeting behaviour is important for coaching people to be more efficient with their time. If confrontations arise, resolve them as soon as possible after the meeting with the protagonists. Luckily, you will not have to handle these difficult participants all at once – well, very rarely.

◆ to use the group. They will have been driven mad by this hijacking behaviour as much as you. Ask for their support in advance and for their feedback in the meeting. They will be delighted that someone is willing to take up the challenge.

◆ to use the meetings checklist below, certainly at the beginning, to keep you on track and remind you of good practice. You may want to give it to the group so they can rate the meeting at the end and feel involved in the whole process.

MEETINGS CHECKLIST

Check

1. Do I have clear objectives for the meeting? ☐
2. Have I invited and briefed the right participants? ☐
3. Have I prepared an agenda and distributed it in advance of the meeting? ☐
4. Remember to arrive early enough to check arrangements. ☐
5. Remember to start the meeting promptly. ☐
6. Remember to follow the agenda. ☐
7. Remember to manage time and finish the meeting on time ☐
8. Remember to involve everyone. ☐
9. How will I help resolve conflict? ☐
10. How will I maintain proper control of the discussion? ☐
11. Remember to summarise decisions as we go and clarify any action to be taken at the end. ☐
12. Remember to prepare and distribute minutes of the meeting within four days. ☐
13. Remember to request evaluative feedback from participants. ☐
14. Remember to carry out agreed actions. ☐
15. Remember to act as a progress chaser on actions to be taken by others. ☐
16. How will I make this meeting fun? ☐
17. What issues will we brainstorm? ☐
18. What other things should I do? ☐

GENDER DIFFERENCES AT WORK

Meetings will also reveal differences between men and women. With increasing numbers of women in the workplace, men are having to find ways of dealing with issues arising from diversity. In the book *He and She*, Cris Evatt talks of 60 differences between the sexes. Here is a selection of some you might come across in the workplace:

◆ **Women tend to be more 'other focused', men 'self-focused'.** This is because women are orientated towards people rather than tasks. It does, however, have the effect of making them rather better team players than men.

◆ **Men do what they please more often whereas women seek approval from others**. In the workplace, the effect of this is that women need to be encouraged to seek promotion. The opposite tends to be true for men. They may have to be persuaded more often that they might require more experience before asking for that pay rise or promotion. So if companies want more diversity at the top of their organisation, they will have to institute mentoring to encourage their fast-track female executives.

◆ **Men tend to express their anger, women to repress it.** As a manager you will tend to know when a male member of staff is angry. Not so with women. You will have to watch out for differences in body language, tone of voice or words used during debate.

◆ **Women tend to be cooperative, men competitive.** In evolutionary terms, winning fights did not give women a reproductive advantage. Quite the opposite, in fact, as men did not find them attractive. Nowadays women often cloak their competitiveness in warmth and friendliness but are increasingly competitive nevertheless.

◆ **Men are more decisive than women.** Because women are people-focused, they want to include others in the decision-making process. They also like to talk through ideas and solutions, not wanting to be given answers, but relying on the talking-through process to help them reach conclusions. This difference has often been misconstrued at work, with women being accused of weakness and poor leadership.

◆ **Men indulge in more verbal put-downs than women.** Women will self-deprecate, men undermine. It is important to understand this difference so that offence will not be taken. Men's competitiveness seems to fuel this behaviour. A woman who can deal with this with a light touch will win the day. Of course, if it becomes harassment, a more assertive approach will be necessary.

Renée Carayol, who wrote *Corporate Voodoo*, says, 'The more diverse the team, the more diverse the thinking and the more innovative the outcomes.' If top teams are all male, middle-class Anglo Saxons, aged 50 to 65, then that organisation is more likely to become hidebound, appealing to a very limited sector of the populace. And since keeping in touch with the customer is the rallying cry of today, it would be foolish if no-one on the board actually understood the customer's standpoint.

'Vive la différence' should be the cry in the workplace. If it isn't in yours, find somewhere that it is.

CONFIDENCE TRICKS FOR STUNNING BUSINESS PRESENTATIONS

Now let us take a look at presentations – a word that strikes fear into many otherwise fearless hearts. I have assembled some advice to help you enjoy making your mark on the business platform.

1: BE YOURSELF

Formality in business presentations is old hat. People want to stay awake and be entertained as much at work as anywhere else, so there is no need to be anything other than yourself. Forget standing behind a lectern, reading your well-honed sentences. Just chat.

2: INVOLVE THE AUDIENCE

I have found that if I involve the audience early on, a number of things happen:

◆ It deflects the spotlight from me.

◆ They loosen up and feel they can ask questions openly, no matter what size the audience.

◆ It equalises the relationship so I am not the one pontificating.

◆ It keeps them awake.

◆ I get to know them.

I had been to Fife in Scotland to address an audience of about 150 people, all business leaders, about creativity in communication. The beginning had not been wonderful, with a prize-giving ceremony during which the compere got most of the prize winners' names and companies wrong. He was a fat man whose shirt oozed out of his waistband, giving the audience an unpalatable view of rubbery white flesh. I suppose there was a certain edginess in wondering what part of his anatomy would be revealed next, but apart from that, the introduction to the seminar was dire. So when I bounced onto the stage to do my bit, they all just stared at me impassively.

It would have been easy to blame the warm-up act or vilify the Fifers, as they are collectively called, but when I analysed my presentation I had forgotten to involve the audience right at the start. I generally ask them to discuss something in groups or pairs, ask me questions or just discuss objectives for the seminar. In my eagerness to get started, I forgot my own advice and it took much longer for them to enjoy themselves.

3: USE MIND MAPS

You will have gathered by now that I don't just *like* Mind Maps, I see them as a way of life. For each speech or talk I do I will use a Mind Map. I rarely reuse one, even for the same presentation, as all audiences are different and I use the Mind Map to focus on their specific needs.

A Mind Map releases you from reading your notes, guides you as to what comes next and keeps you focused on the spoken, not the written, word. I was speaking at a Women in Business conference recently which was introduced by a rather striking baroness. She was young and enthusiastic – not the kind of thing one associates with her title. However, she just read out her speech. I think what she was saying might have been interesting but the written word is not for presentations. We stop listening after a few minutes as we cannot remember the syntax used for written sentences. She also used statistics, but I can't remember what they were as she used no visuals. If she had spent five minutes putting half a dozen slides together and then just chatted about them, we would have adored her *and* remembered her message.

4: USE CASE STUDIES AND STORIES

Great speakers use stories to highlight presentation points. Don't get me wrong, facts are important; but the story will be remembered long after your statistics are well past their sell-by date.

They do not have to be jokes or snappy one-liners; just what has happened to some of your ideas in practice. All to the good if they are humorous, but they do not have to be.

I was taking to a psychiatrist friend recently about the power of the story and contemplating whether storytelling crossed all cultural boundaries. He had recently heard of a colleague in Korea who had started a workshop by asking the audience to contribute stories about things that had gone awry in the communication with their patients. Now, in Korea the practice of medicine is very autocratic and hierarchical. Showing mastery is of supreme importance and loss of face disastrous. However, the stories came tumbling out, and at the end of the workshop everyone said the storytelling had been the highlight. The experiences of others had helped make them feel less isolated and realise that others had communication challenges too.

5: RELAX

I do not believe in all this butterflies flying in formation stuff that consultants tell their clients. For me it is simple: the more relaxed you are, the better you will be as a presenter. End of story.

If you are anxious, you are more concerned about your own physiology than the audience and your impact on it. You should be constantly monitoring how alive they are to your ideas, looking around at each member, noting body language or any inattention. You can then change direction, move to another item or ask questions and involve them more.

Use any trick in the book to relax. Everyone should know these skills. Buy a relaxation tape/CD. There are lots on the market but if you can't find a good one, e-mail me and I will send you one of mine. The advantages of relaxation go way beyond presentation skills. When you are relaxed you are:

◆ focused on others, forgetting yourself.

◆ more creative and able to problem-solve more quickly.

◆ better at vocal projection because of better breathing.

◆ more humorous.

◆ able to get to sleep more quickly and achieve a deeper sleep even before a big presentation.

◆ more likely to live longer and feel better. Recent research has revealed that people who sleep more deeply live longer than their insomniac counterparts. They are also healthier, succumbing to fewer illnesses.

I have worked out some **relaxation tricks** to use before and during a presentation. Try some of these to discover what suits you.

First, I slow down my breathing using the **power minute.** This is what you do:

Close your eyes and count the number of breaths you take in one minute. In and out constitutes one breath. A normal resting breathing rate is around 10 to 12. If you took more than that, you need to slow down your breathing on a regular basis. The relaxation response is about breathing out more slowly, getting rid of that stale air in our lungs, letting go and releasing any muscles that might be held taut. Try the power minute again, breathing in more slowly and breathing out more slowly while sinking into the chair.

If you were attached to any biofeedback equipment (which monitors your nervous system), you would hear a different tone or see a different configuration. Or if you had placed a biodot on a pulse point it should have changed colour to denote that you are warmer. In that short time you will have relaxed, ready to face your audience, ready to deal with anything that might arise.

During the presentation, I never stand behind the lectern and I always ask for the room to be brightly lit so that I can see everyone and their responses. To relax, I might sit on the edge of the table or the back of a chair or walk among the audience. Walking about dissipates any nervous energy that might still be lingering even after relaxing. And a moving target is more stimulating than a static one.

6: DARE TO LOOK DIFFERENT

You do not have to look like everyone else in the company, but there are some essentials for an **appearance makeover** that will help you make an impact:

◆ Invest in a good haircut. This advice is as pertinent for men as for women. If you want to make an impact on a daily basis you can't afford a bad hair day. Go for a cut every five weeks and make sure you can handle your hair easily afterwards. What a waste of time to be looking in mirrors and worrying about how you come across.

I was coaching a man from a large multinational who had aspirations to become a director but who simply did not look the part. He had straggly, thin hair that flopped down over his collar and a straight fringe that looked as if he had been using shears to cut it. The effect was quite unappetising and kind of 60s' hippy. I took him to my hairdresser and he very reluctantly agreed to her cutting his hair. She styled it off his face and cut it short at the back. The difference was staggering. It was the talk of the office the next day, and even the chief executive mentioned it at the board meeting. His rise was swift.

◆ If you are going to spend money on one item of clothing, it should be an expensive jacket for women and a suit for men. Even if you are working in a dotcom company, you will need a suit at some time – a visit to the bank or a conference presentation. Make it a good one that fits well. Women can economise on skirts, blouses and shoes but the jacket has my vote. A good, uncrushable material will mean you can look good throughout the day and into the evening if necessary. Women can get away with bright colours, so go for it. If presenting at a conference, women can get noticed by challenging the grey pinstripes with a red jacket. Men often have to make do with a bright tie.

7: BE ENTHUSIASTIC

If you can't be enthusiastic about your area of expertise, product or company, then hand the presentation over to someone else. Audiences, by and large, want you to succeed and they warm to someone who clearly loves what they do. That is so much more important than having perfect slides or making no mistakes. Mistakes are unimportant; recovery is key.

We all know by now that body language is compelling communication. For presentations, the smile is the most important element. It captivates.

8: ENJOY

Presentations should be fun. And what could be better than to put forward your ideas and have people hanging on your every word?

A **mind game** I use is to visualise every stage of the presentation. Opening remarks with the audience alert and laughing, the argument with everyone contributing comments, then the snappy conclusion with the sound of applause at the end.

I might even imagine people telling me that this was the best presentation they had ever heard me give. I am then ready to enjoy the process.

9: EVALUATE

After every presentation, congratulate yourself for what went well but also ask yourself how you could have been even better. I always try at least one new idea in a talk. It might be a new story, a new slide or a new audience-involvement technique. If it bombs I might tweak it or ditch it entirely. Do not be afraid to ask someone who heard you for feedback.

Ask what bits they preferred to see if it matches with your perceptions.

10: VOLUNTEER

The more you speak, the better you will become, so volunteer for any presentation going.

Now, you may decide that working in a traditional company is not for you. Certainly Max McKeown, author of *Unshrink*, believes that organisations shrink people rather than grow them. They demand conformity and see people as head count and resource, not as a rich seam of contribution and inventiveness. You may come to the conclusion that you have to leave to fulfil your potential.

I know from my own experience that we can stay far longer than we should with a company that has ceased to view us positively. Try the questionnaire below to determine whether it is time for you to stay or move on.

ENERGY RATING SCALE

In response to the following questions, ask yourself whether you feel involved, at the 10 end of the spectrum, or distant, at the 1 end, and whether you are exhilarated (10) or irritated (1).

How do you feel about what your organisation is doing?

Involved	10	9	8	7	6	5	4	3	2	1	Distant
Exhilarated	10	9	8	7	6	5	4	3	2	1	Irritated

How do you feel about how your organisation operates internally?

| Involved | 10 | 9 | 8 | 7 | 6 | 5 | 4 | 3 | 2 | 1 | Distant |
| Exhilarated | 10 | 9 | 8 | 7 | 6 | 5 | 4 | 3 | 2 | 1 | Irritated |

How do you feel about your current tasks?

| Involved | 10 | 9 | 8 | 7 | 6 | 5 | 4 | 3 | 2 | 1 | Distant |
| Exhilarated | 10 | 9 | 8 | 7 | 6 | 5 | 4 | 3 | 2 | 1 | Irritated |

How do you feel about how you are managed in your organisation?

| Involved | 10 | 9 | 8 | 7 | 6 | 5 | 4 | 3 | 2 | 1 | Distant |
| Exhilarated | 10 | 9 | 8 | 7 | 6 | 5 | 4 | 3 | 2 | 1 | Irritated |

How do feel about your colleagues in your organisation?

| Involved | 10 | 9 | 8 | 7 | 6 | 5 | 4 | 3 | 2 | 1 | Distant |
| Exhilarated | 10 | 9 | 8 | 7 | 6 | 5 | 4 | 3 | 2 | 1 | Irritated |

How energised are you today about working in your organisation?

| Involved | 10 | 9 | 8 | 7 | 6 | 5 | 4 | 3 | 2 | 1 | Distant |
| Exhilarated | 10 | 9 | 8 | 7 | 6 | 5 | 4 | 3 | 2 | 1 | Irritated |

If you have scored under 5 on both dimensions for more than one question but less than four, perhaps you should at least start the process of looking elsewhere and/or talk to a boss or manager and ask for some new challenges.

Low energy is often the first sign that you are less than happy with your current circumstances. You do not need to put up with it. Your body and mind are telling you that you are worth more than this. We are often in denial as we drag ourselves out of bed in the morning, citing many others in the same plight. Focus on you.

If you have scored under 5 on both dimensions for four or more questions, dig for freedom. You are more than likely stressed by working in a place that upsets you and saps your energy.

SETTING UP YOUR OWN BUSINESS

One option you may want to consider is setting up your own business. Perhaps you are overworked and have ceased to have a balanced life. It could also be that you have worked out that you would be better running your own company if you want to make money that has no ceiling.

Again, there are sex differences among entrepreneurs. Men take more risks when they start a new venture but their failure rate is higher. Women are often happy with a kitchen/spare bedroom company when they should really go for investment and growth. But they have more persistence and longevity than male entrepreneurs.

Complete the following checklist to find out if you have got what it takes.

TO BE OR NOT TO BE... AN ENTREPRENEUR

1. Do you like to be in charge of your working life?
2. Do you enjoy being independent in your decision making?
3. Do want to put your personal stamp on a product or service?
4. Is security low on your list of motivators?
5. Are you prepared to learn a lot of new skills?
6. Is your family supportive of you going into business for yourself?
7. Can you cut back financially when necessary?
8. Can you cope with the peaks and troughs of business?
9. Are you prepared to work long hours?
10. Are you sufficiently adaptable to do what it takes to meet a deadline?
11. Do you have a vision of where you want to take your business idea?
12. Can you get on with a wide variety of people?
13. Are you prepared to be customer-focused?
14. Can you sell your idea and/or your product enthusiastically?
15. Can you relinquish control and delegate to others?

If you have answered more questions with yes than with no, you can move on to the next stage. Try some of the following:

GOING IT ALONE TRICKS

◆ **Take time** while you are employed to think through your business idea. You do not have to resign in a flounce then worry how you are going to pay the rent or mortgage. Some enlightened companies will help you by giving you time off to set up your company. You will know whether yours fits into that category. Like me you may want to start your business while you are still at work, building it gradually till it can sustain you financially.

◆ **Seek professional advice**. There is so much information out there on websites and at business links. They will direct you to funding, business angels who might want to invest in you and other start up advice.

◆ **Join associations** that will put you in touch with other business start-ups and entrepreneurs who have been through the start-up process. They will provide invaluable help and a shoulder to cry on if necessary.

◆ **Learn to network** but do it properly. I love to meet people rather than see them as some kind of business fodder. If they like you and then discover what you do, they will ask for more information. Frantic selling at network groups is off-putting and has the reverse effect.

I told you earlier about the baroness who opened a conference at which I was speaking. Well, she had just left the platform with the conference organisers when a woman jumped sideways in front of her, thrusting her business card into the baroness's hand. After her leap of

Olympic proportions, she then breathlessly tried to sell her alternative therapy company to this poor woman, who was on her way back to Parliament for a debate. What was she doing? Did she think this strategy would work?

It certainly produced hysterical laughter in the bar afterwards but I'm sure this was not the effect she wanted. Full marks to her for trying, but networking is about relationship-forming, not crass selling. Avoid desperation at all costs.

SUMMARY

So, in summary, choose a good company to work with, stand up and be counted, volunteer for projects, do not be 'shrunk' and go for promotion but be prepared to leave to progress to better things in another organisation or your own company.

TEN-SECOND CONFIDENCE TRICKS

◆ Become visible. Talk quietly about your successes.
◆ Ask yourself 'what would make work fun right now?'
◆ When tempted to moan, write down five ideas for change and talk to someone to make them happen.
◆ Take ten seconds to visualise success when presenting at a meeting. Specifically, visualise handshakes and compliments.
◆ Look for the good points in your boss and reward them when they happen.

◆ Take ten seconds to say thank you to a colleague for a job well done.

◆ It takes ten seconds to volunteer for a project.

Now write your **confidence boosting action plan** as you review the chapter for the tricks that will help you.

LAST THOUGHTS

I do hope you have enjoyed dipping into *The Ultimate Book of Confidence Tricks* and that you have used some of the tricks on offer. We often think of confidence as being necessary for the big things in life but everyday interactions are just as important.

I was reminded of this recently at a conference where I was invited to speak. The topic was Confidence in Business. One women I spoke to at the break told me what her role was in her company. She said 'I just do the easy stuff. Others do the finances and the planning, which is all so much harder.'

She looked good, had an engaging manner and I am sure captivated the customers – which is probably more than the accountant or the planner could do. Why do we underplay our talents? I suppose we live with them and therefore take them for granted. This business woman had never asked for a pay rise or promotion because she had downgraded her contribution to the company on a daily basis. So the small everyday voice in our heads can limit our progression to the bigger picture.

Another example happened when I went with some friends for the first time to a mid-week cinema screening of the more arty Hollywood output. We were seated expectantly at 7.00 pm, ready for the adverts and forthcoming attractions. I love all of that. But nothing happened. Fifteen minutes went by with still nothing on the screen.

We decided to go outside to speak to a manager, who phoned the projectionist. He addressed us from the stage, revealing that the screening time on his agenda was 7.30 and apologising for the error. A member of the audience then said that she had been coming every Tuesday for the past four years and the film had always been late. It occurred to me that all these people had sat waiting for that movie to commence without saying anything and for four years the projectionist had thought the film started at 7.30, not 7.00. No-one had complained in all that time so nothing changed. So the moral of this story is, if you don't speak up, how can others know what you are thinking or feeling?

Telling ourselves we are worth doing worthwhile tasks, and questioning when things do not meet with our approval, is the everyday stuff of confidence.

Also there is no age barrier to trying new things and meeting new people.

Christine, a friend of mine, was invited to the Dorchester Hotel to have supper with another friend and her aunt, who was 88. They were already enjoying a glass of champagne prior to the meal and listening to the resident jazz band in the bar as Christine arrived. A few minutes after her arrival a bottle of champage appeared and the waiter told them that a gentleman at another table had sent it over. Simultaneously the two friends thought that their womanly charms had inspired this gesture, Christine especially believing that he must have seen her entrance. But as they looked over, much to their chagrin, the gentleman in question was clearly toasting auntie. He paid their supper bill as well and left a message for the 88-year-old aunt asking for a date and applauding her obvious delight in the music.

Isn't it good to know that it is never too late.

FURTHER READING AND RESOURCES

Attributions in Action (1999) by Anthony G. Munton, Joanne Silvester, Peter Stratton and Helga Hanks, Wiley West Sussex

Being Happy (1996) by Andrew Matthews, Media Masters Singapore

Body Language (1997) by Allan Pease, Sheldon Press London

Confidence in Just Seven Days (2000) by Ros Taylor with Dr. Sandra Scott and Roy Leighton, Vermillion London

Corporate Voodoo (2001) by Renee Carayol and David Firth, Capstone Publishing

Emotional Intelligence (1996) by Daniel Goleman, Bloomsbury London

Fast Track to the Top (2002) by Ros Taylor and John Humphrey, Kogan Page London

He and She (1992) by Cris Evatt, Conari Press California

Learned Optimism (1998) by Martin Seligman, Pocket Books Non Fiction

Mars and Venus in the Bedroom (1995) by John Gray Harper Collins London

Naked at Interview (1994) by Burton Jay Nadler, Wiley New York, Hodder & Stoughton London

Running Board Meetings (1997) by Patrick Dunne, Kogan Page London

Tackling Tough Interview Questions (1999) by Mo Shapiro and Alison Straw

The Elephant and the Flea (2001) by Charles Handy, Hutchison London

The power of Self Esteem (1994) by Samuel A. Cypert, American Management Association New York

The Mind Map Book (2000) Tony Buzan, BBC Consumer Books

The Sickening Mind (1997) by Paul Martin, HarperCollins London

Time to Think (2002) by Nancy Kline, Ward Lock London

Unshrink (2002) by Max McKeown and Philip Whiteley, Prentice Hall (Business)

Why Men Don't Listen and Women Can't Read Maps (2001) by Allan and Barbara Pease, Orion Books London

INTERESTING WEB SITES

www.bbc.co.uk/health/getconfident

www.bbc.co.uk/lifestyle

www.bbc.co.uk/features/dealing_with_stress

www.rostaylor.com

CDs

MUSCLE RELAXATION by Ros Taylor

If you are experiencing difficulty with sleeping, tension headaches or muscle strain this is the CD for you. It contains 20 minutes of deep relaxation concentrating on all major muscle groups and a further ten minutes of quick relaxation where you speedily wind down and chill out.

VISUALISATION AND PROBLEM SOLVING by Ros Taylor

This CD taps into our ability to imagine. Visualisation relaxes mentally and physically and takes us away from the tensions of daily living. Additionally, this CD helps you to visualise positive outcomes so that problem solving becomes as automatic as breathing.

To purchase either of the above, email: info@rostaylor.com.

CONFIDENCE COACHING

For a package of three half-day sessions of one-to-one coaching to increase personal confidence, call Ros Taylor Ltd on 020 7231 3659 or email: info@rostaylor.com.